QUEST FOR HOPE

[Signature]

ROMANS 12:12

"REJOICE IN HOPE!"

MARK CRABER

ISBN 979-8-88751-967-8 (paperback)
ISBN 979-8-88943-635-5 (hardcover)
ISBN 979-8-88751-968-5 (digital)

Copyright © 2023 by Mark Craber

All rights reserved. No part of this publication may be reproduced, distributed, or transmitted in any form or by any means, including photocopying, recording, or other electronic or mechanical methods without the prior written permission of the publisher. For permission requests, solicit the publisher via the address below.

Christian Faith Publishing
832 Park Avenue
Meadville, PA 16335
www.christianfaithpublishing.com

Printed in the United States of America

Hope (verb)

1. To want something to happen or be true
2. To desire with expectation of obtainment or fulfillment
3. To expect with confidence

Hope (noun)

1. Someone or something on which hopes are centered

Contents

Acknowledgments vii
Preface..ix
Chapter 1:   The Move...1
Chapter 2:   The Blowout 6
Chapter 3:   How Low Can You Go....................................10
Chapter 4:   Hope through Loss..18
Chapter 5:   Really?..24
Chapter 6:   Houston, We Have a Problem 37
Chapter 7:   God Winks...41
Chapter 8:   New Connections...45
Chapter 9:   Rock Bottom...48
Chapter 10: Miraculous Revelation 54
Chapter 11: Leap of Faith 57
Chapter 12: The Doctor Will See You Now.......................60
Chapter 13: In God's Hands..65
Chapter 14: Restoration of Hope...73
Chapter 15: Stacy's Reflections on Her Personal Quest for Hope ...78

Acknowledgments

Special thanks and recognition to the following persons whose hearts were tugged by the Holy Spirit and made this publication possible:

Boyd "Doc" and Debbie Mills
Pat and Pam Murray
Norman and Judy Ditrich
Sharon Gilmore
Bill and Maria Fahey
David and Rhonda Bedee

Preface

In whom do you place your hope? Maybe you have hoped for an outcome in a specific situation and never really thought about the destiny of that thought. The very definition of hope is *a feeling of expectation* and desire for a certain thing to happen. In other words, it's a feeling of trust that something is going to happen, or someone is going to do something—*hoping*—for a good result. I don't know of too many people who would *hope* for a negative result in a certain situation, especially concerning themselves.

When we *hope* for something, to whom are we entrusting our *hope*? Man or God? Where you stand on faith will have a definite impact on how you would answer that question. I know where I firmly stand; my faith and *hope* are in God, His Son, and His Word. With the strength of this trio, my loving resolute wife and son; and a host of many angels, I would not be writing about this miracle of His lifesaving *hope* and His answer to prayers.

We have no *hope* apart from Christ. "Let us fix our eyes on Jesus, the author and perfecter of our faith, who for the joy set before Him, endured the cross" (see Hebrews 12:1–2 ESV).

CHAPTER 1

The Move

In 2013, I was diagnosed with gastroparesis (GP). GP is a chronic condition where the stomach is paralyzed, therefore robbing the body of nutrients from consumed food. My body had eaten over sixty pounds of muscle off my small 5'9" frame. Looking in the mirror after a shower represented a winner of a *Biggest Loser* episode with all the sagging skin. Although God brought us the formula for surviving this disease, my future looked humanly uncertain.

Stacy, my wife of thirty-one years, and I looked at our present financial situation and prayed for discernment concerning our future. We each felt led separately through the Holy Spirit to move to Oklahoma and live on land owned by Stacy's sister. Some of our closest Christian friends and church family questioned this sudden strong commitment to go where we felt God leading us. Even my father and stepmother could not understand the driving force behind our drastic move. The move served two purposes concerning our future. First, it would allow us to live as cheaply as possible because our main source of income was my social security disability (SSD). Second, since we both believed what doctors and research had informed us that without Western medicine intervention, I would not likely survive the GP.

At the time, there were only two treatments for GP: inserting and living off a feeding tube for life or inserting a stomach pacemaker/stimulator in my body to restore its function to normal. Without medical insurance at the time, we did not qualify for either. The medical industry did not know much about GP but seemed certain it could not be treated by diet alone. We felt God was telling us to move Stacy closer to her family for emotional support in the event of my death, which seemed imminent. Both reasons made perfect logical sense at the time, but God had an additional purpose for our relocation unbeknown to us.

I continued the God-provided liquid diet of homeopathic broths and organic fruit smoothies to provide nutrition for my body throughout the move. God miraculously provided help for us all during the move because I was of little to no use being so weakened by the loss of weight. Stacy's sister, Marilyn, graciously provided a small travel trailer for us to live in until we decided on our more permanent residence.

Once we were situated in the trailer, one morning, we both had a *Green Acres* moment. Moving from Houston, Texas, to Kenefic, Oklahoma (down a four-mile dirt road, mind you), would qualify as one of those times when you say, "Wow!" The urgency of providing a home for Stacy was my first and only priority. We just simply could not take much time to shop because the energy burned was too much for me to risk. Everywhere we went, Stacy drove us, and I utilized motorized carts or did not go inside with her.

Quickly, we purchased a small single-wide mobile home to set up on Marilyn's property near Kenefic. Because the location of the home was in the middle of a hayfield, we had to start from nothing to provide the utilities (rural water, electrical, and sewage). I did all I could to help get our new home operational as soon as possible. At times pushing myself ahead no matter how I truly felt, I wanted to expedite the setup of our homestead before I was incapable of physical activity. Getting Stacy established was my priority.

During the process of the move and establishing our home, blister-like bumps started developing on my head, face, neck, and shoulders. Direct sunlight agitated the blisters and made them multiply. We just "chalked them up" to my body detoxing from the GP liquid diet I was consuming for over two years. This symptom was the first sign of a hidden life-threatening issue showing its "ugly-headed" existence.

Even though the bumps were bothersome and a nuisance, we introduced solid foods into my diet, and weight magically started appearing on my thin stickman-like frame. There was not much muscle left on my bones after losing over sixty pounds and weighing in at 129. Gaining a little bit of weight made me feel almost normal again after being down and weakened for so long. I started to help my sister-in-law Marilyn with small projects around the property that had been neglected and put off for a variety of reasons. Marilyn purchased a 1974 Ford tractor with a mower attachment for keeping the land clear to reduce the population of insects and small unwanted critters. Living in the middle of a field brings a whole new perspective to the thought of scattering wildlife when opening the door. That was the first time in my life being that close to a tractor, much less operating it. I've been a city boy my whole life and had never really been introduced to country living.

Also, while growing up in the big city of Houston, my family always had a community trash collection. I was taught at a very young age to be very cautious and careful not to let any legible personal information be thrown away where someone else could steal it. So we brought two paper shredders with us on the move. But Marilyn has lived on this property for over twenty years and always burned the trash, so now we burn ours too. At sixty years young, burning trash is another first for me. The shredders collected dust and were given away due to lack of use.

Since contracting GP and feeling so very useless for almost three years, getting outside and burning energy doing things made me feel helpful and useful again. I could burn calories now and not be concerned about losing weight. For the next few months, the feeling of normalcy started to creep in as more activity ensued, and it felt good. Mind you, there were plenty of very hot baths to soothe sore muscles along the way. Overall, my body was responding positively to the increased physical activity, and the only exception were the blisters, for now.

They multiplied at an alarming rate when exposed to the sun for longer than about thirty minutes. After a day of mowing, my shoulders and neck resembled someone suffering from shingles or even leprosy. It was not a pretty site, and I felt the shame of needing to cover up so others would not think I was diseased and/or contagious. Once out of direct sunlight for several days, the blisters slowly decreased in intensity. Stacy and I started to believe we may be able to beat the life-threatening and crippling effects of GP and survive. God was faithful to bring the liquid diet to us, and our commitment and dedication to continue it was reaping lifesaving returns.

When we sold our house in Houston and relocated, we left behind our son. Markus was twenty-five at the time and had a steady job and a longtime girlfriend. He was attempting to survive on his own in Houston working two jobs to keep his relationship intact. We had been living in our tiny mobile home (896 square feet) for a year and adjusting to our new life. But God had other plans because He knew what was upcoming in the extremely near future for the Craber family.

Markus was struggling to make ends meet, and his relationship with his girlfriend slowly dissolved. The lease for his apartment was expiring, and with much prayer, we made a family decision to move him to Oklahoma to stay with us. All of us had thought that the move was just for a year until he could "get on his feet" financially. However, we had no idea that his role in future events would prove vital as I fought for my life.

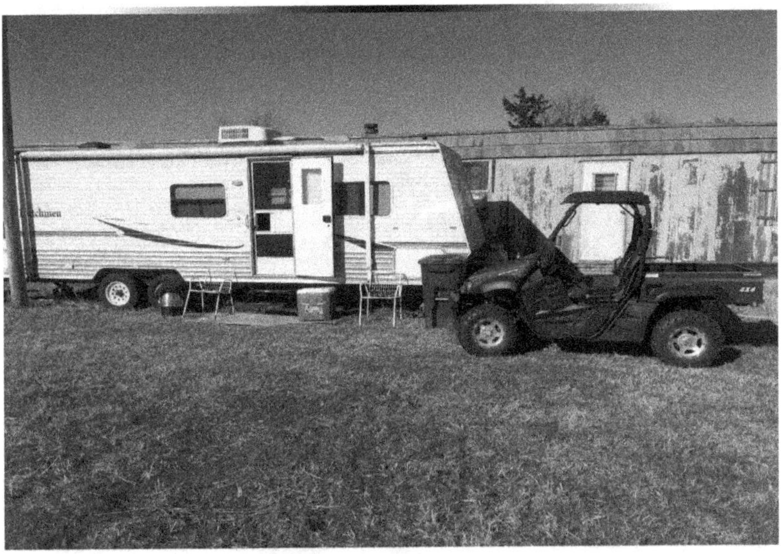

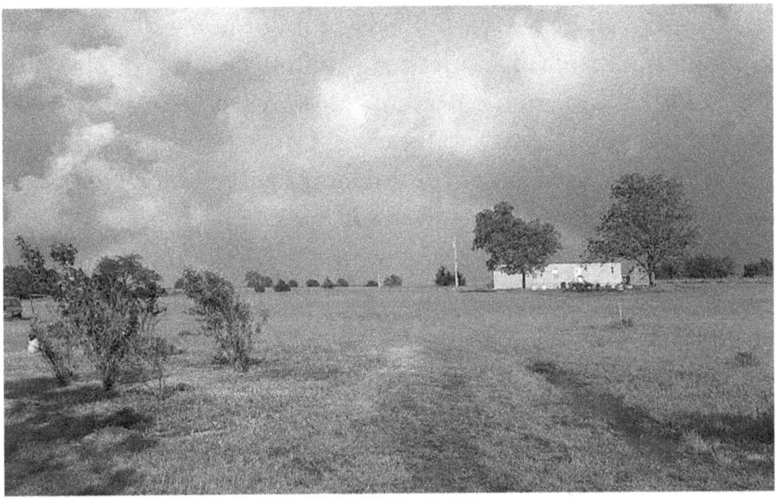

CHAPTER 2

The Blowout

Everything was going great, and we were praising God for healing my paralyzed stomach. Now, we had ideas of creating our little "Eden" in Kenefic, Oklahoma. Thoughts of a garden, fruit trees, a chicken coup, and front/back porches for our home started to flood our minds. I researched and started planning how we could save and afford to build our "home heaven." However, plans are always subject to change or delay without notice. I once heard a Christian say, "When we plan, God laughs!" I do not really know about that, but I do know God's plans for our lives *will* happen.

During a strenuous day of working on the property, I felt a *twinge* in my back. Of course, I just thought a muscle had been pulled; but after two weeks, the pain gradually increased, and numbness started setting in on my right side above the beltline. Either my body was too frail and beat up from many years of physical abuse, or God was trying to slow me down for life-course adjustment, and to the emergency room we went.

I will not go into major detail about this trip to the ER/hospital because the entirety of the visit/stay was pleasant. This was our first time to experience the level of care at this facility, which is locally known as the most trusted place to seek medical care. There are two points I will make concerning this short stint in the hospital to eventually perform a simple spinal discectomy. The first is that most doctors do not really *listen* to their patients. Whether good or bad, most of today's patients are WebMD or Google-informed and know substantially more than patients of the past. They know their bodies better and may really be able to help in diagnosing problems and illnesses. Most doctors after just hearing a fragment of a patient's complaints already have a diagnosis in mind and a prescription pad in hand.

When I worked as an electrician, I had a previous discectomy performed after blowing out a disk in my lower back. Personal experience is golden information and should carry some weight, especially in the ER. As per the usual protocol, the ER did bloodwork and a CT scan. Since they did not see anything glaring digestively causing my pain, they were making plans to send me home. Stacy and I had both informed all medical personnel at the beginning and all through the ER visit that we believed the pain stemmed from my back (spine). With all the commotion and chaos occurring in a hospital ER, sometimes it is difficult to be heard.

"Send him home," she overheard the ER doctor say.

"I don't think so," immediately came out of Stacy's mouth. "You can't send us home without knowing what's wrong with my husband," she said in a very stern demanding voice.

He disgustingly walked away along with the nurse, and we were left in suspended animation wondering about the next step when neither one returned. The next thing we knew, a GI doctor appeared in the room and said there were some spots on my liver that need further testing. Now he had our eyes wide open and ears at full attention and proceeded to say that the spots could be a tumor or cancer, and they were going to admit me for further testing.

Upon hearing the *C* word, he could see the shock on our faces as our hearts simultaneously hit the floor, and he left the room to put in the orders. As the door shut, we both looked at each other and said, "WAIT!" We both knew what the liver *spots* were because of the previous testing performed during the diagnosis of GP; they were hemangiomas. Liver hemangiomas are like blood blisters and usually are harmless and require no treatment, unless they grow too large and start causing pain.

This brings me to the second point concerning this hospital visit. If possible, always have an advocate with you on any medical visit to a doctor or hospital. Four caring ears are essential in making proper decisions regarding the treatment of the patient because two of the ears are in pain and full of medications. So the patient's decision-making process is compromised, and their sole thought is for the pain to just go away.

In today's fast-paced medical processes, a patient cannot fully rely on a medical professional's due diligence when it comes to their body and life. Doctors and nurses are humans who can make mistakes. If Stacy would not have been my observant advocate and spoken up, we could have left the ER with no answers, and my pain would have gone on for who knows how long. A service of care is being provided at an excessive cost so to ensure a patient gets the best possible care. Bring an advocate with you.

In the end, with our influence and many prayers, we finally had the right doctor enter the room. He was "just what the doctor ordered"—a neurosurgeon. This was the first doctor in my life to say that patients know their bodies better than medical professionals, and he ordered a magnetic resonance image (MRI) of my spine. The scan showed a blown-out disk in my middle back; so he performed a discectomy, and I went home the following day. In the weeks ahead, while my body was trying to heal, something inside of me was brewing that I had never experienced before in my life.

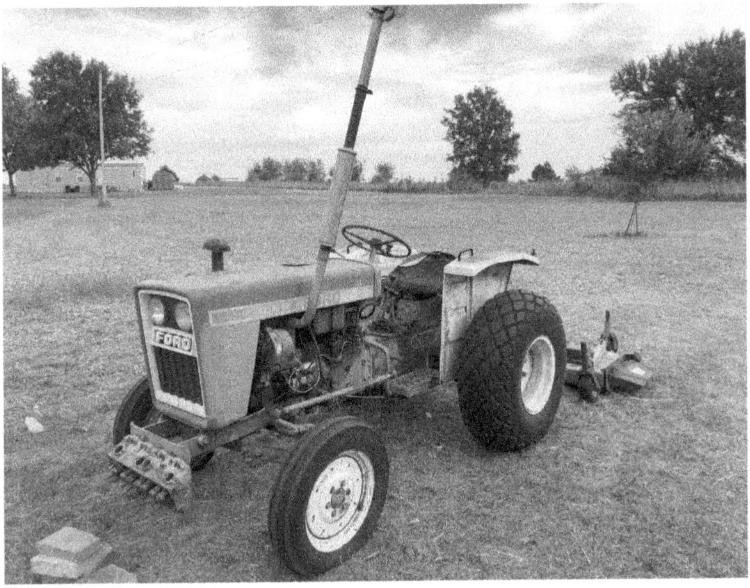
FORD

CHAPTER 3

How Low Can You Go

One morning, like in the movie the *Body Snatchers*, I felt as if my body had been replaced with another version of me. A switch went "on" inside of me that had never been seen or heard of before. Unbeknownst to us was the source of the switch. When it happened, I did not even know what to call it because I had never experienced *depression*. During my life, especially recently, there have been many reasons for me to be depressed, and Satan knew it. The list was very long of all the things that were lost in the last few years: job/livelihood, loss of business, intimacy, health, home, savings, and retirement. To lose any one of these causes many people to fall into a self-defeating depression. The evil one used every single one of these and more to attack me and take away my zest and joy for life.

The loss of money and livelihood hit my core being as a man because I could not provide the standard of living that we were accustomed to for most of our marriage. The disability payments were providing enough for us to survive. The company Stacy and I had started from scratch and ran for fourteen years was broken apart and sold. It crushed me to be forced to give up my pride and joy and the pinnacle of my career. We were in a mobile home on land we did not own in the middle of nowhere and had no retirement or savings left.

After thirty-five years of marriage, everything we had built up was gone. The hope of rebuilding anything faded away into a dark tunnel with no source of light to be found. Inheritance is not a big deal to our son, Markus, but I really intended to leave him more than just some life insurance.

These are examples of how negatively my brain was functioning because of what Satan was feeding me. Negativity always destroys hope, and in my mind, there was no positive outcome for a productive future. The attack of my manliness did not stop as I spiraled downward into darkness and despair.

Stacy and I have been married for over three decades and love each other intensely; like all marriages, our times of intimacy have had their ups and downs, no pun intended. Because of the diet I was on while fighting GP, there was something about the combination of nutrients that reinforced my libido. We were both pleasantly surprised by the increased physical activity and felt blessed by God. It was the only exercise my body was getting, and we joked about making sure I got in my physical therapy and cardio workout.

When the switch was turned on with the depression, something else was also switched off in my head—the *desire* for intimacy. It is not that my equipment did not operate, there wasn't a spark or urge to use it. Stacy knew something weird was going on because of the sudden loss of desire, but she just included it with my many symptoms of depression. This was the biggest hit to my existence as a man, and Satan really started hitting me with everything in his arsenal.

My earthly existence and future looked bleak, and my *hope* and faith were being truly tested. As a Christian, Jesus has secured my eternal future. But as months went by, cry-praying started to become a nightly routine. "Why, Lord?" became my sole focus as negativity intensified and anger began to enter the mix. The inner voice in my head kept telling me I was a failure and that the only way to help my family and improve their lives was with my life insurance.

Raising Markus was my purpose, and now it was over. I was no longer useful to anyone being disabled and depressed. About six months into the self-punishing depression, signs appeared that left people close to me wondering whether living was important to me anymore. My speech, actions, and demeanor prompted even Stacy to start to question a promise I made to her after my brother David's suicide.

Throughout the many years of marriage, I have made numerous promises, and I have tried my best to keep every single one. As I was starting the fight for survival from GP, David gave up his fight to be pain-free by committing suicide. His groin nerve pain was excruciating and debilitating. David was a strong Christian who helped many with his kindness and love of people. We both really loved to help and serve others, but neither of us was physically capable any longer. Our paths were remarkably similar at the time, and we were both praying for healing.

Shortly after his death as we were all reeling from the tragedy, I made her a promise. The promise was to *not* go out like that and take my own life—to not give up! The damage done to me and the family by such a life exit was devastating and unrepairable; it left a horrendous scar on our hearts that will never completely heal. Stacy trusted me and had faith that I would keep my promise because I had never broken one before, and I am a man of my word. And my love for her was unbreakable, and she knew it. The regret of making that promise would haunt me many times during the remainder of this season of depression and the fight ahead I would face of lost hope.

The negativity I was feeling fed the seed of anger, and now the depression had taken full control of my life. My treatment of others, including family members, was totally unlike the "Mark" they knew and loved. I was confrontational and argumentative at any given moment on any topic. The aura around me was infected with the lies Satan and my brain had conjured up together. It was as if some evil villain had infiltrated my head, and I had lost control of my brain. The more I thought about my unfortunate past occurrences, the angrier I became. My *hopeless* situation was consuming every second of my brain function. It really did not matter who was in front of me; my negativity and anger spared no one.

As the saying goes, "We sometimes hurt the ones we love the most." It is absolutely true. Our closest family seemed to always receive our happiest of highs and our lousiest of lows; however, for me, there were no present happy times. When close family expressed concerned, everything in my verbally abusive arsenal was available because I knew they loved me the most. The family events or gatherings I attended were a challenge for everyone concerned because they knew what they were going to get—an angry, bitter, negative, and depressed human.

I will never forget what Stacy said to me during one of my angry "I wish I were dead" outbursts: "I just want my husband back. You know, the man I married." She was right. I was a different person. Deep down inside, I knew something was seriously wrong with my thought process, and I was out of control. My subconscious even decided to relinquish my handgun to Stacy one afternoon after an unprovoked emotional eruption. Stacy was very confused by this and started to wonder who this person was in front of her because she knew my deep personal conviction of never using a handgun on myself. Besides being depressed, something underlying had to be causing my drastic change of personality. But what?

My nightly cry-prayers turned into begging God to take me home to heaven in my sleep. I did not like who I had become and no longer wanted to be alive. When a person does not like themselves, it is difficult for anyone else to like them. Pretty soon, I just stopped trying to take care of myself by not eating and neglecting my overall hygiene. To prevent confrontation or hostility, Stacy would make gentle reminders to brush my teeth and take showers. Her patience was wearing thin, and she was hoping and praying I would break out of it and return to my old self.

As my depressed state escalated, she convinced me to see a local family doctor for possible medical help. We had already tried natural and homeopathic remedies for depression with no success. Since the move, we had not seen a local doctor for anything. My past dealings with "Western medicine" doctors and Big Pharma had not been beneficial to my health, so I was not very enthusiastic.

We were pleasantly surprised by the doctor's friendly country demeanor and open attitude toward alternative medicines. He was extremely easy to talk to, and I began to unload my recent baggage on him. Once he heard a fraction of my rant and the nonprescription medications we had tried, he suggested using antidepressants. I did not like popping chemical pills, but my attitude was at an all-time low, and I was willing to try anything.

Antidepressants are widely used and prescribed by medical professionals in the United States. One in six Americans takes psychiatric drugs, mostly antidepressants. There are hundreds of varieties at a wide range of costs. Our budget could not take a big hit from any area, so my family doctor limited his selection to the lower cost and more-often used medications.

For the next few months, the doctor tried four different antidepressants to help slow down the crippling effects that the depression was having on my life. One after the other was attempted, and each brought its own undesirable side effects. These medicines did not provide any relief to my depressive state but did add unwanted headaches and nausea, which made me feel worse and, in turn, enhanced the negativity and anger. Stacy, the doctor, and I were all very shocked that none of the medications worked and decided not to pursue alternative more-expensive medicines. After a discussion of potential insurance-approved treatments, the group consensus was to investigate counseling.

Counseling or therapy is a touchy subject for Stacy and me as a couple. We tried *secular* marriage counseling in our distant past and did not like their *worldly* approach to solving relationship differences or difficulties. Most of it was more about revenge than forgiveness and more about self than others. We both would prefer a Christian counselor and/or pastor over any other options. At this time, neither was available, so I researched for nearby Medicare-approved counselors. There were none, and the closest was over sixty miles away one-way.

Tammy, an overly concerned close friend from high school, offered to pay up to five hundred dollars for the much-needed therapy. We had been communicating more recently because she was troubled about me and did not like what she was hearing me say. The words I used and the sound of my voice left her feeling my life was in dangerous territory.

After several weeks, I finally reached out to a male counselor and made the call. I felt a male counselor could understand the losses to my manhood better than a female. After a brief conversation, he believed I needed long-term help and decided five visits (one hundred dollars/visit) would not be enough time to make considerable progress in my depression. He offered to locate a closer counselor or social worker who would accept Medicare. A brief time later, he sent me the name of the one in the area. I immediately called and made an appointment. The only issue for me was that the counselor was a woman.

At this point, it was a blessing just to be able to talk with someone other than Stacy and Markus. I just kept telling myself, "Beggars cannot be choosers." After four weekly visits, the communication was good for me; however, there was no significant improvement in my downheartedness and hopelessness.

My view of life was deteriorating rapidly, and Stacy knew something needed to change for me spiritually. We had tried everything we thought was available to us, and nothing turned my negative view in a positive direction. We had been attending a local church that was not feeding our deep internal spiritual need and desire for intimate Christian fellowship and love. Stacy had overheard some mothers at the daycare where she worked talking about a new church in the area. Fusion Bible was meeting in a school until they could move into their newly constructed facility in a couple of months. Stacy was determined to get me there, and we attended the next Sunday's service. God knew exactly what I needed now and how much more we were going to need the Fusion body of believers soon.

Even in my state of desolation, I knew this was where we were supposed to be from the first visit. As soon as we entered the school building, a bald gentleman wearing a volunteer T-shirt promptly welcomed us to Fusion in a very friendly manner. The service was quite different because it was totally dedicated to prayer. We were surprised to see the man who greeted us was the lead/senior pastor. They prayed for the community, their new building, and several other things. But the one that impressed me the most was when they prayed for other churches in the area. It spoke volumes to me and said plenty about a church's identity when they know they are not the only "song and dance in town" that preaches the gospel and wins souls for Christ.

As we exited the auditorium, the pastor was engaged in conversation with another couple, but upon seeing us, he made a point to stop and invite us back as we left. We both felt uplifted on the way back home. Stacy knew her prayers had been answered for our new church home, and *hopefully*, there would be help for her very mentally broken husband.

One of the requirements of the church is to be in a small group, called a D-group (discipleship group) in order to connect with the church body on a deeper level and make new friends. One Sunday, God found a way to introduce us to a D-group leader, and we attended their next scheduled gathering. The first meeting was great for me because they let me unload bottled-up emotions and feelings. When the meeting concluded and most of the attendees departed, two couples stayed after and stood outside with us listening to me spew my guts for an hour. It was the longest conversation I have had with another male in several years. For the very first time in over a year, an actual good feeling came over my body. We now had a D-group to attend weekly as God knew we would need this fellowship of Christians to support us now and in the months to come.

This positive spiritual uplift was making a dent in my impenetrable depression. My prayers for God to end my worldly misery were slowly fading away. On the other hand, in the weeks during this spiritual awakening, a familiar nagging discomfort had developed in my right upper abdomen. The last time this type of annoyance occurred, it led to a gallbladder removal in 2011. Distant memories of doctors, hospitals, numerous medical tests, and pain flooded my thoughts. This discomfort was in the exact same location as in the past but acted a little different because it appeared intermittently, which made it a nuisance.

Like most small pains, we hope they will disappear and go away and just not worsen. From one day to the next, I never knew how my day was going to go until I got out of bed and started moving around. My sleeping habits were not really being affected for some strange reason. Once my body was horizontal and still, the discomfort seemed to drift asleep just like myself.

Along with the discomfort, little red bumps began to appear on my chest, stomach, and right arm. In the following weeks, these red bumps grew in number and turned into a full-blown rash. The source of the epidemic baffled Stacy and me because this was my very first time experiencing a breakout and/or reaction of this nature to anything. Also, rashes were usually caused by the skin encountering a substance the body is allergic to or does not tolerate. The cause of my rash baffled us because I rarely even left home, and there was not any "rolling in the hay" naked. Most rashes have a *pattern* that suggests the possible cause or origin. This rash resembled no other, and a few of the sores were very painful and some even bled. Red dots started appearing on my bed sheets overnight, causing us to search my body for the source the next morning.

We tried baths, lotions, homeopathic remedies, and Benadryl, yet nothing treated it with success. The only other symptom that accompanied the rash was the discomfort, which after several months was growing into pain. Stacy and I believed the rash and pain were connected somehow; we just could not fathom the struggle and journey to reveal the answer that would almost destroy our hope.

CHAPTER

4

Hope through Loss

With the depression ongoing, the onset of a new mysterious health concern was the one thing that was not needed—another tribulation. My stepmother called and informed me that my dad, who had been in the hospital fighting sepsis among other illnesses, was being placed on hospice care at home. Fred was eighty-seven years old and in the final stage of his life, and he knew it. Dee, my stepmother, revealed that his leukemia resurfaced its ugly head which was brought on by the sepsis. The doctors only gave him a couple of weeks to a couple of months of life remaining on earth. Our relationship never truly had a chance to develop into a bonding father-son closeness. There simply was not very much personal private one-on-one connection time. At the age of one, my adoptive parents divorced, and visitation with my dad throughout my childhood was sparse at best.

Even though she would never ask, Dee was going to need help with the initial setup for him and getting the house prepared for caring for him. Feelings for my dad and stepmom overwhelmed my depressive state. My inner thoughts that were focused only on myself were overruled by the inevitable loss of my dad. God placed in my heart the desire to assist them in any way I could, but that would mean traveling to Kingwood, Texas, and we did not have the funds.

I put it off for a few days, and God's calling turned into a rock concert on Sunday morning. At church, God arranged a quick private conversation with our D-group leader where I asked for prayers for my dad. He knew of our financial situation and graciously offered to donate toward my travel expenses. All I could do was cry and look toward the heavens, thanking the Lord for His provision. He knew the desires of my heart, and they fell in line with His plans. Now I could make the call to Dee with the plan to be of service that God had given me.

From the sound of her shaky frightful voice, I could tell she was worried about losing him. She kept saying the words, "Your daddy," in about every sentence, so it really made me feel as though she could use the help and support. Without her saying it, the message was received that it could be my last time to see him. Having been married for thirty-eight years, they did absolutely everything together and cherished each other immensely. Neither genuinely wanted to live without the other as with many blessed long-lived godly marriages. She was totally worn out from the numerous trips back and forth to the hospital and rehabilitation facility for the past ten weeks. She would have just stayed with Fred all the time if it were not for their children, Bucky and Bobo, two Bichons.

Thanks to an angel's generosity, I was able to go and spend a week assisting and visiting them. Dee suggested Stacy not come accompany me because Fred would be uncomfortable with another woman in the house. It was exceedingly difficult for Dee and the nurses to clean him up and perform other medical necessities with his clothes on, so he was only wearing a hospital gown and socks. Also, he could not get out of bed or walk and needed a hoist to be moved.

When I laid my eyes upon him and we hugged, my heart and soul were crying out loud internally without even a hint of outward expression. It frightened me when his upper body cracked audibly upon the hug. I could feel it, and the thought of hurting him scared me. He was simply a stickman of just bones and skin; there were just traces of muscle left. A person would never know how bad he really was if they could hear him converse. He had made his peace with God about his long life and was ready to go home. The joy of knowing his destination gave him an indescribable but explainable countenance. He lived his life free of anger and knew the joy of laughter even as his independence and dignity were slowly being stripped away. There were even some sounds of laughter as we three were hoisting Daddy from the bedroom to the living room chair.

Under the circumstances, the trip was highly successful in aiding Dee in getting him set up at home. Despite my health issues, the relief provided to Dee and the fellowship with Daddy boosted his moral. The change in his attitude was so noticeable to Dee that she called me a couple of days later to ask me to come back in two weeks. God knew what my dad and I needed, so He called upon the same angel to bless us again with funds to make another trip to Houston. However, this trip would be drastically altered by yet another heart-tugging event.

On the first night of the second trip, a phone call informed me that my mother was in ICU at the hospital and would not survive the night. Honestly, I was not surprised or shocked about my mother. She had full-blown dementia, and she did not speak, walk, or recognize her own son. I had said my goodbyes to her more than five years ago. We did not have the best of relationship because she was always more concerned about herself than anyone else. Not having a dad for the entirety of my childhood hurt the development of my adopted brother, Paul, and myself.

When confronted, my mother would never come clean with me and tell the truth regarding her past, and it negatively consumed her conscience. It made her terribly angry and bitter toward the end of her life, and she took it out on the ones she loved the most—Stacy and me. The Lord and I had forgiven her, but she could not forgive herself. Sadly, she did not make it throughout the night, and I could not be with her when she passed even though she would not have known it anyway.

Now much of the time at my dad's house was spent making final preparations for my mother. Being her only remaining child and no spouse for the last thirty-five years, all arrangements were left up to me. She had no close family, so there was no need for a funeral and/or service. Her ridiculously small life insurance could not cover a burial, so cremation was the only viable option. It broke my heart that we could not afford to assist in the burial she would have preferred.

God used the Houston traffic, which is horrible at any time, to distract my mind from dwelling on her wishes as I drove all over town to manage my mother's final affairs. There were still plenty of quality-time moments with Daddy; however, his decline was progressing rapidly. I can vividly remember the last time I saw him, kissed him, and hugged his frail body, but I chose not to fix that vision in my mind for my final memory of him.

Two weeks to the day that my mother passed, the call came from sobbing and mourning Dee that Daddy's pain had ended, and the Lord had called him home. The proper grieving for my parents was not instantaneous because my focus was distracted by "brain fog," and the intensity of the pain was increasing. To this day, I really do not know if I ever *grieved* for them because, in my mind, seeing them again is a certainty.

There were lessons learned through the process of losing both parents. Firstly, it is selfish, but I would rather have a relationship and fellowship with loved ones in their final stage of life. My mother lost her mind through dementia, and for the last five years of her life, there was zero communication. My dad lost his body, but we could reminisce about the past for hours and laugh. I know which one I would prefer, so I asked the Lord to please spare my mind from brain-altering diseases. Secondly, my mother displayed childish anger because she would not accept her circumstances which were from her own choices and attitude. She acted very bitter toward the world and wanted a do-over. Daddy had an opposite *hope* view and was content with his life journey and knew where he was going—he was ready. God knew I would need to be reminded of this *hope* in the health battle ahead. Also, having this kind of faith during the last days of my life would encourage others through a powerful testimony of the *hope* found through Christ's love and salvation.

The difficult heart issue for me was that neither of my parents had a funeral service, and they were both cremated. It just went against traditions followed while growing up in the baby boomer generation. With the costs of funerals and burials on the rise, cremation has become the choice of many today. Dee did have a memorial service for Daddy at their church, which Stacy and I attended. The loss of both so closely together did not help my depression, and the pain intensified from my heavy heart. My nightly prayers used the word *why?* numerous times as they turned into cries out to God in my distress.

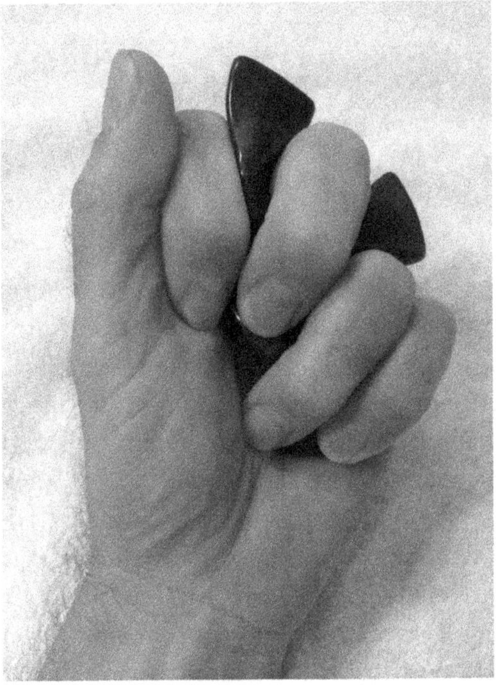

CHAPTER

5

Really?

God used Fusion and the D-group to strengthen me spiritually and emotionally because He knew the weapons needed to encourage me in the continued fight out of my depression—and now grief. Because I was now concentrating on the pain and rash, my brain resources had little room for energy spent on gloomy unpleasant thoughts. However, my anxiety was growing because the thought of seeing *any* doctor for a mysterious pain brought back very displeasing memories. Over-the-counter medications were no longer masking the pain, and maximum-per-day limits were a pill away. At least I liked the new family doctor, so that was a positive. The next doctor visit would start a series of events that led to a multitude of tests, specialists, hospitals, and medical *hopelessness*.

When the doctor revisited my recent medical issues concerning my bile duct, he ordered bloodwork and prescribed a two-week supply of pain medication (hydrocodone). The bloodwork would show any sign of infection, but the main area of interest was the liver and pancreas enzymes because of the pain location. He was overly cautious not to give me a large quantity of pain medication because of my recent severely depressive behavior. We returned in two weeks for the blood test results and a refill. Nothing in the bloodwork pointed to the cause of the pain, and all numbers were in the normal range. So he referred me to a gastroenterologist (GI) doctor.

In today's Western medicine/insurance system, a patient cannot just show up at a specialist's office without a referral from their family physician. This is because the insurance company will not pay because they did not have a chance to approve or disprove the doctor's visit—crazy stuff. The referral was to the same GI doctor who saw me briefly when I had the back surgery. The wait to see this doctor was six weeks. I remembered this phrase used very often in the oilfield, "Hurry up and wait!" While feeling *put off* for having to stay in pain longer, the six weeks seemed like a weekend on the beach compared to the suffering ahead.

The last pill of my most recent pain medication supply was taken the morning of the GI doctor's appointment. The first encounter with this doctor was much more pleasurable than this experience. When he entered the room, he greeted us as if we were part of a crowd of people as he walked by shaking hands. He nonchalantly listened to my past medical story about having the almost exact same pain that took an endoscopic retrograde cholangiopancreatography (ERCP) in Houston to repair several years ago.

An ERCP is a specific type of endoscopy where a GI doctor can explore past the stomach into the duodenum and perform certain procedures on the common bile duct (CBD). Then he looked at my bloodwork results and, without any other information, said, "You don't have a bile duct issue." He wanted me to get computed tomography (CT) scan of the abdomen. The CT scan is a sophisticated X-ray that would provide detailed images of my internal organs to look for abnormalities. He quickly shook our hands again and said his assistant would manage us next with the details.

His assistant informed us it would take a week to get the CT scan accomplished. Since my last pain pill was taken earlier, I requested enough pain medication to make it until the test results come in. She instantly responded, "Oh, the doctor *never* gives pain medication to his patients!"

"Just because I saw the doctor didn't make my pain disappear," I replied.

"I'm sorry. If you can find some place to do it quicker, that would help," she said.

Trying not to cause a major scene, I sternly grunted, "Sorry does me no good!" and stormed out of the office and sat in the office building hallway in disgust. Stacy apologized on my behalf and settled the bill, and we went home as I sat in silent outrage.

Everyone is different when it comes to utilizing acetaminophen (Tylenol), ibuprofen, and opioids. For me, acetaminophen works for fever, and ibuprofen helps me with headaches and very minor aches. Anything more serious requires opioids to dull my brain senses to the existing hurt. Any doctor who disregards a patient's pain is doing a disservice to his profession and his oath. However, pain medications should not be handed out like candy as has been done in the past.

Once we returned home, the pain medications gradually wore off, and the pain sharpened more intensely and turned into a stabbing pain. Popping Advil like candy throughout the night, I barely slept. A heating pad did not help, and no position was comfortable. Early on Thursday morning when my family doctor's office opened, I phoned them to request a refill. In the meantime, Stacy was feverishly calling around to find someone who could do the CT scan sooner. The doctor's office returned my call an hour later and informed me that since I had seen the GI doctor, they could not refill my pain meds without an appointment. It would be four more days before he could see me.

To be honest, I started to question God a little at this point, saying, *"Really?"* Both doctors had left me no choice but to go to the ER; suffering for several more days was not an option for me. The pain was drastically increasing, and my emotions were in overdrive. Stacy had found a medical testing center that would do the CT scan on Friday, but waiting that long seemed unbearable.

Stacy, trying to stay strong, frantically loaded me up, and we headed to the ER. She was starting to worry because she could see the pain on my face and the nonstop kicking of my legs as they were hitting the car door repeatedly on the way. Her anxiety was building as she drove, so she relied on her "go-to" in times of stress. Christian music filled the air waves as she began to pray aloud. God knew she needed support, so He prompted her to call Markus to let him know

QUEST FOR HOPE

what was happening with his dad. Markus had left earlier that day to help a close friend in Houston. He was not very far away because of traffic and immediately turned around to come back to the hospital. He arrived before we did because he was genuinely concerned and drives like his "old man."

We were *hoping* for a similar conclusion to this ER visit as we had on the first trip to this hospital. The stabbing pain was excruciating as I moaned and chair-squirmed in the ER waiting room. They got me back and into a trauma room in a decent amount of time. God bless the nursing staff; they did their best to try to calm me down, but nothing was stopping my legs from wildly moving around and kicking. It took them two attempts to insert the IV, and Markus had to lie down on my legs to hold them still on the second jab. I simply could not communicate my current health condition coherently until they finally injected some Zofran and morphine into me to calm my pain down. Morphine causes some people to become nauseated, so Zofran is commonly used along with it. We informed the ER doctor of the visit with the GI doctor and the CT scan that was ordered but not yet performed. In short order, they wheeled me out for a CT scan, and by now, the pain had diminished enough so I could cooperate and follow instructions.

While the testing was going on, Stacy was desperately seeking prayers through social media from family, friends, Fusion Bible, and our new D-group family. When I returned to the room, she tried to cheer me up by showing me the quick responses from the many people praying for us. My anxiety was calmed by the outpouring of support and, along with the morphine, allowed me to relax enough to close my eyes. The ER doctor returned to say the CT scan did not uncover a cause for my pain, and they were going to admit me for further testing. We were all relieved to know my pain was going to be managed, and *hopefully*, they were going to find a cause and solution to my pain.

The hospital put me on the cardiac/stroke floor because of the lack of available rooms on the GI floor. The very first thing I noticed was that the bed made a horrible air compressor pumping noise and moved every few seconds. Morphine was scheduled every four hours, and my focus was to ensure their promptness to keep the schedule. When someone is in pain, their sole purpose and goal is to relieve the pain—almost at all costs. The sharpness of the pain I was experiencing was mostly subdued by the round-the-clock morphine, so sleeping should not have been an issue. However, there was an air compressor running on the underside of my bed every seven to eight seconds, so it was incredibly difficult to fall asleep. It is hard enough to sleep in a hospital with the temp/BP checks every four hours, and the noisy bed made it even harder.

The reason for these types of beds on this floor is that the patients using them do not get up and walk from the bed very often, which causes bed sores. The bed moves rhythmically every few minutes to minimize the potential skin irritations.

Sleep was just not going to happen, so I unplugged the bed. To my unpleasant surprise, the upper half of the bed deflated. The nurse informed me afterward that when the bed was unplugged, it should have set off an alarm. God is good because no alarm sounded, and no one knew why—but God did! Now instead of a noisy bed, it was a quiet uncomfortable lopsided bunk with half a mattress. My only option left was to turn around and lie in the fetal position at the foot of the bed, and I did just that. The nurse came in later and decided to leave me alone because slumber had finally overtaken me even if it was for only a couple of hours.

The next morning while I walked *laps* on the floor, I noticed a different style of bed with no air compressor. I returned to the room and found my nurse waiting there to tell me the GI doctor ordered a CT scan with contrast, and they were coming to retrieve me. Pointing to the bed in the hallway with an emoji frowny face, I said, "Please?" She was going to put in a request with maintenance and expedite the swap before I returned from the test. I was overjoyed when I returned because the beds were swapped, and now hopefully, rest would follow. The first night with the new mattress allowed me to sleep so well that I skipped a scheduled pain injection.

Another excuse I used to get the new bed was walking. From past hospital experiences, getting up and walking the floor hallways aided in healing and showed the staff I was healthy enough to leave.

Because no one else was strolling the hallways of the cardiac/stroke floor, I was known as the nursing staff's floor "Walkie-Talkie." If the hallways were not graced with my presence, a person or nurse would come to my room for a chat, knowing Jesus would most likely come up in the conversation.

After a decent night's sleep and some breakfast, I received an amazing phone call that shocked me. It was the senior pastor from Fusion checking on me because someone had told him of my hospital stay. We had only been attending Fusion for a brief time, and I was very impressed by his genuine love and concern for my well-being. After we had talked for a while, he closed with a prayer. This was a call of support for the battle ahead. God's timing for the call was impeccable, as usual.

Soon after the call, the GI doctor entered the room and made his diagnosis declaration regarding my pain issue. His diagnosis did not make logical sense and would not be confirmed by a second opinion. He noted the results of the CT scans stating my bile duct was flowing perfectly, and I had two hemangiomas on my liver, along with two cysts on my kidney. In my mind, I'm thinking that must have been a new and amazing CT scan to see the tiny biliary system. We knew about the hemangiomas, and he said they had not grown since the scan done the previous year. What he said next made Stacy and I start to go down a "rabbit hole" in our brains. He said, "The two cysts on your kidney are the size of lemons, and the displacement of that space inside your body cavity is causing your pain. You do not have a digestive issue, and I'm going to refer you to a urologist. Thank you and goodbye."

He shook both our hands, and he hastily exited the room. We were left in utter amazement and shock. What the heck? Was this life-threatening? We both desperately reached for our phones and started Googling like mad. The sky's the limit when it comes to potential problems related to cysts, growths, or tumors. Neither one of us slept well that night with our minds wondering and wandering. We started praying heavily for a positive experience with the urologist and for Him to calm our racing thoughts and anxiety.

No other doctor entered my room for the remainder of the day. However, God knew what we needed and answered our prayers quickly with surprise visitors. The couple who leads our D-group had come to visit and pray with us. They were shocked to hear about our unusual hospital/doctor experience as they had always heard of good experiences at this hospital. It was a wonderful time of fellowship and prayer, and they encouraged us to try to stay positive. Stacy and I were left feeling the Lord had sent angels to lift our spirits.

Early the next morning, the hospital admitting doctor came in to inform us that they were discharging me. Because all my test results were normal, he was sending me back to my family doctor to reevaluate and re-refer me if needed. The first words out of Stacy's mouth were, "No, you're not!" As the doctor stood in silence, my heart sank in disbelief. Stacy said demandingly, "You are not sending him home without knowing what is causing his pain!"

"What about the urologist?" we both next said in unison.

Then he said apologetically, "The hospital only has one urologist, and he is not taking any new patients. We used to have three, but two left suddenly without notice, and we are searching to replace them very soon. We are going to refer you to a urologist, and you can see him/her as an outpatient."

Now, both of us were getting agitated because we felt like I was being treated like an addict trying to fake pain for drugs. No one likes to be looked upon as an addict or a hypochondriac, especially when their pain is legitimate.

"What about the cysts?" was my next question. He proceeded to tell us the cysts were on my left kidney, not the right as the GI doctor led us to understand. The displacement diagnosis was bogus because we thought pain cannot radiate from one side of the body to the other in the organ area. Up and down, yes, but not left to right, unless severe spinal nerve pain is involved. To say we were both upset would be accurate. We demanded to see a urologist, and I stipulated to never have the GI doctor enter my room again. I am quite sure he felt badgered and quickly left the room to move on to his next (victim) patient.

While he was gone, one of the very friendly nurses entered the room. We could not hold back voicing our displeasure of the current situation to each other and her. Her empathy toward my circumstance was quite calming. She informed us that the hospital had a "patient advocate" (PA) that could assist a patient with these types of occurrences. An advocate's job is to help patients navigate the healthcare landscape and ensure they receive the best care possible. They can also advise them of their insurance rights in hospitals, and mine was Medicare. We asked her for a recommendation of another GI doctor within the hospital for a second opinion, so we had a name to request. Nurses are not supposed to recommend doctors, but she did say most of the nursing staff like working with one specific GI doctor. It is not known for sure, but when she left the room, we believe she made a few inquiries on my behalf.

Less than an hour after the nurse left the room, an advocate was knocking on my door. She was an elderly gray-haired lady who was very pleasant and engaging. Her concern was truly genuine while talking to us about my current lack of care as she scribbled notes all during our conversation. In a subtle way, we demanded to see a urologist because this was the first time we heard of any kidney cysts, and we wanted a professional diagnosis. Also, we aggressively requested a second opinion from another GI doctor and strongly urged a reevaluation from the doctor favored by the nurses. She apologized for our negative experience and left the room to champion for my health. For us, the situation was unsatisfactory with the hospital discharging me with no answer to my pain and basically no direction forward.

During this time of waiting, my thoughts were being flooded with stewing negativity concerning my treatment. As these thoughts were building, I loudly voiced my displeasure with Stacy, and as the intensity was increasing, the phone rang. The senior pastor had called to check in on me and pray with me. It was a Holy Spirit—led phone call because he said just what I needed to hear, and I felt uplifted afterward. The one point of the call that made a significant difference in my life then and now was when he said for me not to "lose my Christianity." He heard the frustration in my voice that could lead to anger and cause my words and actions not to resemble that of a

Christian. With the challenges ahead of me, his words would need to be stored in my heart for future use.

Remarkably, the hospital's attention to my case ramped up after the chat with the PA. In my experience, seeing the admitting doctor more than once a day is a rarity. After a couple of hours had passed, the admitting doctor returned to give us an unusual afternoon update. He had conferred with the sole hospital urologist and discovered the cysts located on my left kidney have not grown since last year's scan. They would not require attention unless left-side pain or other kidney-related symptoms develop. So my right-side pain could not be caused by the cysts. As my suspicions were confirmed regarding the GI doctor, my angriety (anger and anxiety) raised its ugly head and became vocal. My nurse entered the room about the time I yelled, "I do not want to see that *quack* GI doctor come into my room again! He is a moron!" The nurse and the doctor knew from the inflection of the rant that I meant every word. With my angriety escalating again, the doctor slowly crept his way to the door and quickly exited.

After the doctor's cowardly escape, the nurse softly said, "Well, then good because the GI doctor you requested is going to drop by and consult with y'all about your case." God and His angels were working behind the scenes because the nurse knew something was amiss with the previous GI and spoke with the new GI personally. She seemed more invested in my care than the admitting doctor and had an incredibly special calming effect on us. Her *loving devotion* and *compassion* for her craft were evident. For some strange reason, I have always had more favorable nurses than doctors when it comes to compassion for a patient's pain/suffering. Nurses seem to corner the market on possessing a good "bedside manner," and it is because they put these two qualities into their work every day.

A brief time later, there was a knock on the door, and a *kid* in a white coat walked into my room. He was an incredibly young Asian man that looked like he had just walked off the stage after receiving his high school diploma. Stacy and I were shocked to find out he was the consulting GI doctor we requested. He politely greeted us, promptly sat down, and then looked at me and said, "Okay, tell me your story." He stoically sat there for over twenty minutes and heard my whole medical story since 2011, seldomly interrupting for questions or clarification. He did not look at any electronic device or distract himself from being "all-in" to the conversation, barely even taking his eyes off me.

This type of commitment from a doctor, when communicating with a patient at the bedside, is almost nonexistent in today's fast-paced medical industry. As first impressions go, he put forth a stellar performance. After reviewing my records and hearing my medical saga, he decided to get a closer more detailed view of my insides and ordered an MRI with contrast. He said the contrast would help *light up* my organs and abdomen where everything would be visible. We humbly thanked him for taking the time to consult with us. He told us once the MRI results were received, he would return and discuss them.

We believed the test would take place in the morning since it was already late afternoon. To our surprise, the wheelchair arrived to take me for the MRI an hour later. "Wow, that was fast!" Stacy said. Suddenly, we both felt like ever since we spoke with the patient advocate, attention to my ill health increased substantially. An MRI is an extremely isolating and deafening test to endure, but having pain medication in my system aided in reducing the anxiety. It must be a horrible experience for someone who is claustrophobic or has phonophobia. I'm very grateful for headphones and the ability to close my eyes and drift away to the sound of classic rock-and-roll music.

Throughout the evening, we both did a substantial amount of *hoping* and praying that a solution to my pain would be obtained from the results of the test. Surely with the expertise of Western medicine on their side and my insides lit up, the radiologist and/or doctor would see something abnormal to repair. The previous scans did not reveal any signs of cancer or tumors, so we were confident and thankful for not being shocked tomorrow with any life-threatening news. I just knew this test was going to expose the source of my pain, so my spirits were up, and a good night's sleep was in order.

After breakfast, there was a light knock on the door, and in walked two white coats. It was the admitting doctor and the second

GI doctor at the same time. When more than one doctor is in a hospital room, something important is about to take place. My smile when they entered the room soon turned into an emotional frown. The GI began to tell us that the results of the MRI were normal, and in fact, all tests performed were normal since arriving at the ER. Both doctors were puzzled and stumped as to the origin of my pain and produced no solid conclusions. However, the *kid* GI doctor had a theory pertaining to an extremely rare condition known as sphincter of Oddi dysfunction (SOD). The muscle that allows bile and pancreatic enzymes from the common bile duct to enter the duodenum is called the sphincter. SOD is a medical condition defining that when a muscle goes into spasms, it can cause obstructions in the flow of the bile and enzymes that result in biliary pain. Usually, a sphincterotomy is done to treat the SOD. They had to produce something, and since there were bile duct issues in my past, it sounded reasonable and logical.

Great! So that was good news, right? They had a potential cause; now let us get it repaired. What are you guys standing around for? My brain was in high gear processing these thoughts, and then the GI doctor said, "Now for the good news and the bad news. The good news is that I can perform the necessary ERCP to treat the SOD. The bad news is, the hospital does not have the manometry tool for the ERCP scope to do the sphincterotomy."

Wait, what? The hospital does not have the equipment to do the necessary procedure to relieve my pain. Huh?

At the time, his response made little sense to me. At that point in my life, I had never been to a hospital that did not have what it needed to help and treat people. The GI doctor could see the frustration building on my face and answered my next question before it was asked. As he handed us a slip of paper, he said, "There is a GI doctor in Plano, Texas, who I would personally go to if I needed this done. And since I am only a consultant on your case, I can only recommend you see him. I will communicate with him about your case, so he knows you are coming." The admitting doctor then said he was discharging me and referring me to this new GI doctor.

Stacy and I were stunned by this new development and began discussions immediately upon their departure. We thought since the hospital did not have the necessary equipment, why aren't they transporting me to the hospital of the new doctor to get this done? Why do we have to make the appointment? We were both very discouraged by their lack of urgency for someone in pain and currently on morphine. The same very helpful nurse entered the room at the same time we were considering asking for another meeting with the PA. She could feel the tension in the room and asked us if everything was okay. After expressing our concerns to her, she explained to us who was really in control of those decisions—Medicare. By their rules, insurance would not cover the ambulance trip to a different hospital because my condition was not life-threatening. In a way, it made sense but not to a person in unknown abdominal pain that required morphine.

36

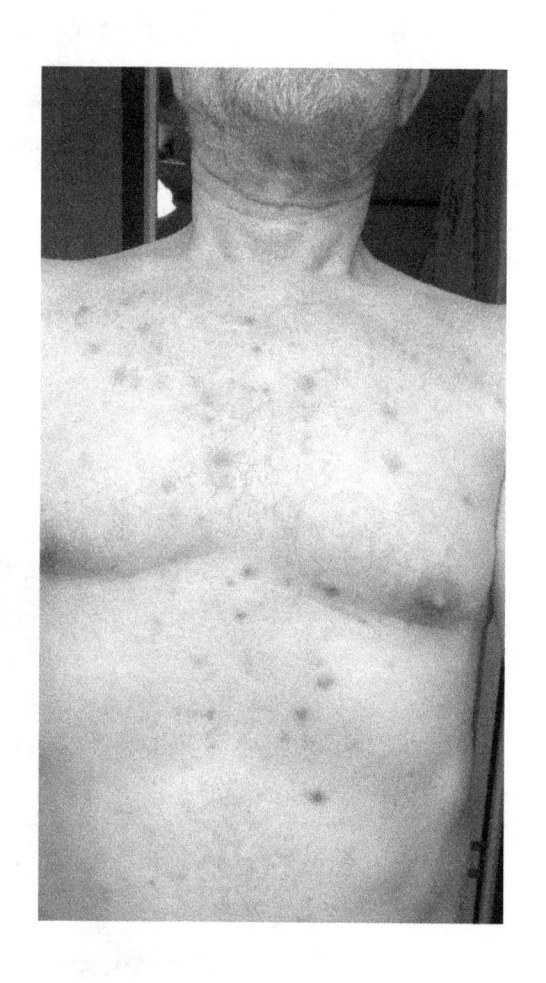

CHAPTER 6

Houston, We Have a Problem

Stacy decided to wait until we got home before trying to communicate with the new Plano doctor's office to set up an appointment. For the next four days, his office's ineptness and playing phone tag forced our hand. We had a potential appointment in sixty days, but they would never call back to confirm, and our patience was very thin. I knew a GI doctor who could do the needed ERCP on me; he was the doctor who repaired my bile duct in 2013. The only problem was his location, Houston, Texas, which is five to six hours away by car. We had little choice, so the call was made. To my amazement, an appointment for next week was achieved instantly.

Now for the problem of accommodations, where were we going to stay with an undetermined checkout date? A hotel would have been extremely expensive, and we would not ask my stepmom because she was eighty-two and in poor health. We had many friends in the area from living there for eighteen years, but there was only one person we would ask for this favor, and that was Tammy. She was considered family and lived near Willis, Texas, on Lake Conroe, which is just north of the Houston metroplex. In our teenage years, Tammy and I lived in the same subdivision, attended the same high school, and carpooled to school most days during my junior year. We have stayed connected throughout the decades, and all three of us have spent many good times together. She has been one of the few friends who I still had in my life from my childhood. We gave her a call, and she was sad to find out about my pain but incredibly happy to help us in our time of need. She was excited to see us for any reason.

We were concerned about running out of pain medication and the long-term effects the pills were having on my diagnosed GP. The duration of our trip to Houston was undetermined, and we discovered that acquiring pain medications from the GI was hit or miss, mostly miss. Believing we had the GP under control and not wanting to regress, pain patches were the only other option. We knew about the patches and could have used them earlier, but they are much more expensive than oral pain meds, and our budget was fixed. My family doctor prescribed a one-month supply of Fentanyl patches just to get me through the ERCP. Fentanyl is a narcotic that is used to treat severe pain and has an elevated risk of addiction and dependence. Stacy would not allow me to drive at any time during our trip to Houston—understandably!

Stacy did a fantastic job driving the whole distance on her own, only taking several stops along the way to rest her back and stretch her legs. With her fibromyalgia and previous back surgery, she cannot sit comfortably for prolonged periods of time. We arrived late Wednesday evening for my doctor's appointment on Thursday, and after that was unknown. The scheduling for the ERCP or other doctor-recommended procedures was totally in God's hands. It could be days, weeks, or months; we were just clinging to our faith and *hope* for a speedy pain remedy.

The doctor's visit was very short, and he agreed to do the ERCP because we had a history. Most GI doctors are cautious in performing them because of the elevated risk of the patient developing pancreatitis. In 2013, he did an emergency "roto-rooter" procedure to open a blocked bile duct. He said he would do the sphincterotomy to treat the SOD and that there could be scar tissue causing the pain as well. Without this past relationship, he would not have done the surgery. Even with the distance we had to travel, we knew God sent us to the right place. The ERCP was scheduled for next week, and I was very thankful for the extended supply of pain patches. The hardest symptom to overcome with the patches was drowsiness, and staying awake for me was a major problem. One week was a pleasant surprise because of the delays we have experienced in the medical industry to this point. Now we had to tell Tammy of our prolonged stay.

Tammy, of course, had no issues with accommodating us until I could travel after the surgery. She has been an *angel* to me throughout our whole relationship. The ERCP was accomplished as an outpatient, as scheduled, and the doctor said he cleaned up a little scar tissue, but the duct really did not look that bad. We were immensely grateful for Tammy's hospitality and could not thank her enough. Two days after surgery, Stacy did another fantastic job getting us back home, and we *hoped* and prayed this was the end to my pain.

When an ERCP is done, the patient is very sore from their internals being manipulated, and the pancreas is the most vulnerable to infection/inflammation. For the next week, it was difficult to determine if the surgery was successful. After two weeks, the pain in my gallbladder area had increased and added another horrible symptom, a stabbing burning sensation. By now, my pain medication needed a refill, so we scheduled yet another appointment with my family doctor.

The doctor changed my pain medication back to hydrocodone because of the trying-to-stay-awake issues and the inherent dangers associated with the long-term use of fentanyl. He received all the information from the Houston doctor and referred me to a specialized GI doctor in Oklahoma City (OKC). He adamantly recommended this doctor as the one he personally would see if he had GI problems. Within a couple of days, we had an appointment for the following week in OKC.

The thing I remember most about this doctor's visit was that I could not pronounce his name. It started with a *V* and continued for thirteen more letters, and he was from Thailand. Dr. V wanted to do another ERCP and utilize an ultrasound to scan for cysts and tumors in the bile duct area. He had diagnosed this type of biliary problem before, and the pain symptoms were like mine. Dr. V performed the ERCP the following week, and he found no tumors or cysts, and he told Stacy everything looked normal. I was too groggy to know the results until we got home, and I was not overjoyed, to say the least. The rash and pain still existed, and both were getting worse with no solutions or diagnosis within reach. It was time to see the family doctor again to refill pain meds and get a new plan.

The family doctor could see the painful frustration on my face, and we had more questions than he had answers. He had another GI specialist for me to see in Plano, Texas. We were to set up the appointment, and he was going to personally speak with him concerning my health. I called the new GI, and the next available appointment was in July, which was four months away. The doctor's scheduler informed me that if a cancelation occurred, their office would call to let us know. I just knew my GP would come back in full force if I continued the pain management regime indefinitely. *Hopefully*, the pain and the source causing the pain would not worsen, and I could last through the pre-appointment waiting time. We just trusted God and requested prayer from anyone and everyone we knew, especially from our church and D-group.

CHAPTER

7

God Winks

One month went by very slowly, and knowing I could not last until the scheduled appointment, I called the doctor's office. The scheduler said there were no cancelations, and if it was an emergency, which it was to me, we should go to the Plano hospital ER and request to have the new GI see me at the hospital. Stacy loaded me up, and we headed out for Plano. We prayed the whole way there for a positive outcome and expectantly *hoped* for a correct diagnosis of the source of my pain.

The ER did the normal protocol of bloodwork, urine test, and a CT scan. We informed the staff of the desired GI doctor and showed them the upper torso rash, which now covered my upper body from the beltline to the neck and right arm. The nurses thought the rash was systemic, instead of being localized by a skin irritant. We agreed with the nurse's assessment, but the doctors would not address the rash at all. Every doctor we had seen to date had not been concerned about the rash or related it to a more complex problem. When we brought it to their attention, they all just said, "You need to go see a dermatologist." The rash was a horrible symptom of a health issue, but the burning and stabbing pain was the priority, and they could be connected. The ER doctor decided to admit me so they could manage my pain and allow the GI doctor to see me.

In the room later that night, the hospital GI doctor came by with the results from the tests. We deflatingly heard yet another, "All tests were normal!" The GI doctor we had an appointment with was with a group of doctors, and someone from that group would come by to see me in the morning. We were comforted, just a little, that another set of eyes looking at my case would reveal a cause. Under morphine pain management, I slept well, ate well (for hospital food that is), and anxiously awaited a new doctor's insight.

After waiting all morning, we finally saw a doctor, but it is the same hospital GI doctor who told us that a doctor from the group would *not* be coming to see me. He also informed us they were discharging me, and I was supposed to keep my scheduled appointment. So the person who answered the requested GI doctor's phone told me wrong, and my family doctor did not communicate with him about my case. Being very distraught, I immediately insisted the nurse remove my IV and told Stacy to "GET ME OUT OF HERE!"

The staff could see how upset we were and tried to hurry us out of there, but it was not fast enough for me. I did not even wait for the wheelchair exit service. The over-an-hour drive home was not pleasant and filled with negativity about what shoulda-coulda-woulda happened. I had to pray for forgiveness once we got home regarding all the pessimistic texts to various people and my gloomy disposition considering my future. I maintained my *hope* and faith in God but had minuscule *hope* or faith in Western medicine. Now we would have to go back to the family doctor to report in and to figure out where we go from here.

This trip to the family doctor was different from the previous visits. We saw a bewilderment look on his face as he had no answers after reviewing all the information provided from the hospital visits and surgeries. He would not refer me to another GI because that avenue had been exhausted. He said, "It is time to think outside of the box" and decided it could be a pinched nerve in my spine causing the pain. I had to get a spinal x-ray and an MRI with contrast so he could rule out nerve pain. The unknown pain was taking its toll on my mind and body, and the doctor could see it. He ordered the nurse to give me a pain shot before we left to help ease my anxiety and pain.

When we were walking out of the exam room, he said, "Hey, you guys come back here and let me pray for y'all." Our family doctor was a Christian, and he knew we were incredibly involved in the local church because we invited him to Sunday services. God knew we needed a spiritual lift from an unorthodox person and industry, so we would know it came from Him. I have never had a western doctor pray for me in my life, so in my mind, this act of sudden spirituality had to come from the Lord.

These occurrences or signs I refer to as "God winks," and I have had many in my life. They are simple reminders that God is watching over our daily lives as we struggle to live on a fallen planet. Ultimately, He is in control, and His plan for our lives will be fulfilled. When we place our *hope* and trust in Him, He guides and signals us with these "God winks" to keep us on track and to let us know He is our life's sentinel. I could not help but feel uplifted as we left the doctor's office.

As the pain shot wore off, reality set in that I could not indefinitely continue the pain pill usage. I was taking the same medication that caused my GP, and we were concerned it would come back in full force. Since Western medicine was not helping me, we turned to alternative treatments for pain.

Acupuncture had worked for Stacy in the past with her fibromyalgia; in fact, it was the only treatment that improved her pain levels. Providers of acupuncture are abundant in the Houston area, so there are many options. But there is only one acupuncturist in Durant and the surrounding area. Four visits to a tiny Asian lady did not produce any noticeable improvement in my pain level. We were living on a fixed income, and Medicare did not cover acupuncture, so we decided to reallocate those out-of-pocket funds for a substitute treatment.

Even during all the doctor and hospital visits and just plain feeling awful, we continued to attend the D-group. We needed spiritual encouragement and communication with like-minded people as we struggled through this season of an unknown illness. Most of the members were kept up to date as to our recent medical struggles, especially when we met, because they could see my pain in front of them every week. They saw the thriving to live, *hope* being slowly drained from my spirit. Western medicine was not helping me, and it was evident to them, so they encouraged us to try anything that could potentially reduce my pain.

At the end of a weekly D-group meeting, the leader decided he wanted to anoint me with oil. Anointing with oil is prescribed by Saint James to be used for the recovery of the sick (James 5:14). Jesus gave power to the twelve disciples to heal the sick by anointing them with oil (Mark 6). The leader, a new Christian and prominent veterinarian in the area, was being led by the Holy Spirit as he had never performed such a ritual. His gesture was perfect because it came from his heart. He genuinely cared, being spirit-led, and had great compassion for God's creations. The group's act and prayers infused me with God's *hope* for a speedy diagnosis of my pain. I had to take a shower and wash my clothes when I returned home, but it was all worth it.

CHAPTER 8

New Connections

During this time of dealing with my unknown health problem, I received a mysterious Facebook message from a stranger. To notice and retrieve a nonfriend message is convoluted and takes effort for someone not familiar with navigating social media platforms. She was a very sweet lady searching for information regarding my adopted brother, Paul, who died in 1993. Paul and I were adopted by different parents, him in 1957 and me in 1960. She had an adopted sister who was interested in her DNA and ancestry. It turned out that Paul and her adopted sister were siblings; they had the same mother. After sending messages to everyone on Facebook who had the name Craber (not very many exist), I was the only person to answer. We started communicating via text, and after a few short weeks, it quickly developed into a close relationship.

Paul and I were adopted from the same agency out of Dallas, Texas. She had obtained the adoption records for Paul, and she offered to assist me with getting mine. This was God's timing because we were considering pursuing my family medical history in search of a possible explanation for my mysterious pain. In the past, when Markus was born, Stacy attempted to get adoption records, but they were sealed by the court, and I was the only person who could open them. Throughout my life, I've never really desired to discover my ancestry because of opening a "Pandora's box." I guess my timidness was due to the unknown having a negative impact on my life. Although I would greatly benefit from knowing my ancestry, we did not gain any medical insight through my blood family. However, God was working behind the scenes to perform a grand lifesaving miracle with the connections made from this association.

As the burning and stabbing pain escalated, it was affecting my whole being. I was ready and willing to try anything to help in alleviating the pain. Medical cannabis had just been approved by voters in Oklahoma, and some D-group members and close friends were telling us to try cannabis to help relieve my pain. Anyone who encountered me could see discomfort and agony on my face.

In my youth, I used cannabis to break away from my unhappiness and to try to feel better about my identity. In the 1970s, cannabis was abundant and inexpensive. It was used by many youths to rebel against the present government and escape their realities. "Partying" filled my teenage years, but like most adolescent rebellious activities, they dissipated with adulthood. Also, back then, we were breaking the laws of the land, and cannabis was totally illegal. Times have changed!

I went to a medical doctor (other than my family doctor because he wasn't licensed for a medical cannabis diagnosis) so I could get medically approved and apply for a card to enable the purchase of legal cannabis. After receiving my card, I purchased some *medicine* at a dispensary specifically grown for intense pain. It helped greatly in two specific areas. First, it allowed me to decrease my daily consumption of pain pills by one per day. Second, consuming cannabis in the evening before bed allowed me to sleep through the night. There was no longer the unpleasant occurrence of waking up in the middle of the night to take a pill and waiting for it to take effect. While cannabis did aid my pain, it could not replace pain pills completely, and we could not afford for me to consume it 24-7. We fervently prayed for a miracle answer as I was slowly getting worse, and Stacy could see the life draining out of me.

The next time I saw the family doctor for a pain med refill, he could see the rapid deterioration of my overall health and well-being. He said there had been many discussions with his dad (he practiced with his dad in the same building) as well as many colleagues about my case, and there was a consensus. There was a new young and very intelligent GI doctor in the area who could offer a revolutionary new approach to my case and hopefully deliver a potential solution.

Once we heard the doctor's name, we both remembered a consultant who was requested at the first hospital visit. He was the doctor that suggested SOD as a diagnosis. The reason we did not continue with this doctor was that the hospital did not have the manometry tool for the ERCP scope to perform a sphincterotomy. Because of all the additional information provided to him from my recent surgeries and doctor's visits, maybe God could use him to figure out what was wrong with me.

Stacy was ready to try just about anything because she could see the life escaping her husband's body ever so slowly. My pain was now moving into the excruciating phase, which negatively affected my appetite and attitude. I just didn't care to eat and wasn't concerned about keeping my body alive. Stacy did her best to keep me *nutrified* with natural supplements and vitamins. I took whatever she gave me without question.

CHAPTER 9

Rock Bottom

The young GI doctor was very shocked to see me in about the same pain as many months ago. After he reviewed my recent records, he made the determination that no more ERCP surgeries were needed because that diagnosing technique had been exhausted, and no problems were exposed. The last resort in diagnosing an unknown pain in the abdomen was to do exploratory surgery. In layman's terms, exploratory surgery is when a surgeon inflates a person's upper torso with air and uses a laparoscope to investigate all organs and surrounding areas for any sign of disease or infection. He gave us two surgeons to choose from, and *we* picked one that was well-known in the area and a Christian. Stacy was now making all my health decisions with very little input from me. Operating on very little brain power, I *hoped* that we were headed in the right direction.

The first visit with the surgeon was quick and mostly unmemorable—to set up the dates for the preoperative physical examination and exploratory surgery. When we were discussing my recent medical history, he concentrated solely on the fact I had GP and how he worked with Medicare to implant stimulators (like a heart pacemaker) for the stomach to treat GP. He solely focused on the steps he would take to get a stimulator installed and ensure that Medicare would cover the costs. He explained the difference between a ninety-minute gastric-emptying scan (GES) and a four-hour GES and told me that I would need the four-hour test to get Medicare to approve the stimulator surgery. I remembered that years ago when my GP was diagnosed, the hospital performed a ninety-minute test, and my results were 0 percent, so there was no need to proceed with a four-hour test.

We both said emphatically in unison, "We are not here for GP!" Stacy was getting a little perturbed now and sternly replied that my GP was under control through diet, and my current pain was not due to the GP. She lifted my shirt and said, "GP isn't causing this!" as she pointed to my rash. At this point, all he could do was agree and move on with performing the exploratory. He refocused and said he was going to investigate every square inch of my insides for the cause of my pain. His certainty of finding the cause was made very evident to us.

As the preop was approaching, the pain moved to another level, and I was randomly vocalizing my pain through involuntary moaning and groaning. The time between pain pills rapidly decreased, and both of us started to wonder if I was going to make it to the surgery date. On the day of the preop, Stacy loaded a hurting moaning man into the backseat and headed to the hospital. We stopped for lunch, and I could barely eat because of the pain. She could not handle seeing me in agony any longer and was alarmed that I could be in mortal danger. Straight to the ER we went as I was weeping in the backseat and fearful of yet another hospital visit.

We both started praying simultaneously as tears streamed down our faces. This trip to the hospital would be one of the record books of my life and, in my opinion, the cause of my medical post-traumatic stress disorder (PTSD).

Stacy informed every medical person we encountered at the ER about missing the preop appointment and the upcoming exploratory surgery with the surgeon's name. We were hoping the surgery could be moved forward, and/or a different surgeon could perform the exploratory. After all, we were at a hospital, and they *hopefully* had more than one surgeon available.

The ER staff decided to admit me under a "pain management" option through Medicare. I would be seeing an admitting doctor once in a room who would determine how to proceed. Behind the scenes, without our knowledge, a test was being ordered early the next morning that would make my night a painful living hell.

Once in the room, my pain was being managed, at first. I was given my normal amount of medication by the nursing staff before seeing any doctor. The nurses were compassionate and kind, as usual, *but* they had to follow the doctor's orders. They leaked the pain *management* regime to us, and it was insufficient to keep me comfortable without screaming out in pain. "I was more comfortable in pain at home than in here," I repeatably yelled out throughout the night. God bless them; they tried everything in the medical and common-sense arsenals to appease me and my pain. Nothing worked! Everyone on my floor and anyone I knew whom I could text knew about my pain, my lack of care, and how I wanted to die. Even my new *family* friends looking for my adopted brother knew. I spared no one near or far on how I felt.

Slowly, the built-up pain medication level from months of continuously popping pills began to decrease, and the pain sensors in my body were on overload. All of us have had moments of serious pain in our lives, but never in my life have I felt this level of pain for this long with no relief in sight. I had always been a pretty good and compliant patient with hospital staff, but this time was very different. I was expressing my displeasure with everything instantly and without any moral reservation or concern for anyone or anything. I was completely out of control and did not resemble who I was in the past. I had very little regard for anyone, including my loving caring wife. My vocal outbursts from excruciating pain even shocked her after being married to her for over thirty-five years. This went on for hours as time sluggishly passed by.

In the past, when I was in pain in a hospital, the usual time frame between morphine pain shots was four hours; now they were telling me twelve hours. They also gave me one pain pill in between the morphine injections. It was totally inadequate to keep me from screaming out for help. We could not understand *why* they were not

QUEST FOR HOPE

managing my pain. The nurse was telling us it was because of an upcoming test but would not inform us of *what* test they were planning on doing, which was activating my angriety.

When a digestive time-related test is done, the doctors do not want the patient on any type of opiates because the test could produce inaccurate results. The opiates slow down the digestive system and adversely affect the test. As the pain shot time approaches, the red help button gets a workout, and the nursing staff gets hounded constantly. They better not be one minute late with my injection.

During the night when pain and darkness filled the room, Stacy was in constant prayer and care mode. She was trying so hard to be strong for me, trying to shield me from her crying. There wasn't much she could do that the nurses missed besides pray, and she sometimes prayed out loud for me to hear. Watching her husband suffer and in complete despair was heartbreaking. There comes a point when a loved one's suffering outweighs the need to hold on to them.

For the first time in our marriage, she was ready to let God have me. She could no longer observe me suffering and pleading for God to take me home. After all, we were *in* a hospital, and her husband of over thirty-five years kept yelling out in pain with very little relief provided. For a Christian, knowing where a loved one is going after they pass away is of great comfort and value. Being mindful that they will see them again is reassuring and uplifting even though they will be missed on earth.

We pleaded for a second opinion, but the hospital was short-staffed on the late shift, and the only other doctor available was the ER doctor. We didn't care; however, we waited for three hours before he came to my room at 3:00 a.m. I had hoped for a lessening of my pain, but all he did was give me a pain steroid, which barely dented my agony. He told us he could do very little because he could not override the *doctor's* orders. The second opinion was of no use, and my opinion of the admitting doctor was at an all-time low, so I couldn't wait to "rip her to shreds" the next time she came to see me.

A knock on the door came around 6:00 a.m. It was a young gentleman pushing a wheelchair. "I'm here to take you to your scan," he said.

"What scan?" we said in unison as he had our full attention now.

"Your gastric-emptying scan," he said.

Now with raised voices, we both said irately, "No, WE ARE NOT DOING A GASTRIC-EMPTYING SCAN!" Although neither of us slept a wink throughout the night, we were both very wide awake now. I was livid, and I yelled at Stacy, "GET ME OUT OF HERE!"

Now everyone on the floor could hear the violent outrage going on in my room whether my door was opened or closed. The nursing staff was urgently calling to get the admitting doctor to my room before something got broken besides me.

Thirty minutes later, the doctor entered the room, and I started my barrage. I have never been ruder to a doctor in my life than I was to her. She ended up leaving the room because she just could not communicate with a crazy man yelling at her, and Stacy followed right behind her. Stacy closed the door and had a lengthy conversation with her outside in the hallway. I don't know everything that was said, but I do know the talk was softer toned; and once Stacy reentered the room, the hospital changed their care for me. Immediately, I was given a morphine injection. Then, Stacy informed me of what the doctor revealed to her.

The doctor whose orders everyone was following was the exploratory surgeon who was pushing the four-hour GES at our first office visit. He was unreachable and out of town but somehow put orders in the system for me while I was there. He ordered the GES test, which only allowed me to receive the very minimum of opiate pain medication so as to not negatively alter the test. I guess at this hospital, a surgeon is somehow a high-ranking doctor, and most other doctors cannot override their orders. Even though other doctors are in front of the patient. We never saw or spoke with the surgeon that whole trip to the hospital.

They were discharging me with pain medication, and I was to make the scheduled exploratory in four days. I finally felt relief from the pain shot, the anger slipped away, and I was coherent enough to understand most of what Stacy said. The nurse brought us two prescriptions for pain: One was for 2 mg Dilaudid and one for 10 mg oxycodone. I was to alternately take them every four hours, but I only had enough to make it to the exploratory surgery. Stacy must have gotten their attention because they understood my pain now.

While we were waiting for the discharge papers, I was updating my newly found family about my situation because it looked grim from my perspective. She told me she had spoken with her sister concerning my recent health issues and that she was sending me an email with a possible clue that could help me. At the time, I was thankful but did not look at the email or understand its importance until we returned home.

Once we were loaded into the car, we both wept. Stacy was spiritually and physically exhausted but still had to drive us home with a few stops. Before she could drive, she prayed because her stress and anxiety were through the roof, and those are never good for a fibromyalgia sufferer, especially without sleep. I was lying down in the back seat, so I could not see her driving, but I remember one thing. Stacy's a good and competent driver who usually has loads of patience and is not aggressive. I have trouble spelling patience and believe it's a "heavenly virtue." She sounded like me driving when I was young yelling at other drivers. I don't know how we got home; we must have been riding on the backs of guardian angels.

We were pretty upset with God and desperately seeking understanding *why* we had to endure such hardships. Our displeasure that Western medicine still had no answers for my pain after sixteen months was made very clear to God through our "scream prayers." Our *hope* for an answer was at an all-time low. Both of us were constantly praying all the way home: Some were silent, most were vocal, and all were tearful.

CHAPTER 10

Miraculous Revelation

Once we arrived at our home, both of us could not actually believe it. Still in the car, we both collapsed in tears and scream-prayed in unity to God for the next fifteen minutes that we both were done. We could not go any further without Him making it perfectly clear which direction to proceed. He and His angelic army would have to carry us the rest of the way because our mere mortal human bodies could not go one more step. Once we finally unloaded our frustrations to God from the car, we went inside and straight to bed. After being awake for over thirty-five hours, we passed out and slept for hours.

We finally felt somewhat human again after waking up from such a lengthy nap, and I wasn't in excruciating pain because of taking such strong pain medication. I opened the email before we even ate anything, and I couldn't believe the revelation we uncovered. The email had an article attached from an OB/GYN doctor in Texas. The doctor wrote about women having serious health issues from a female contraceptive device that was made of titanium. He also mentioned that some women have had health complications resulting in *metal surgical clips* left inside the body after a cholecystectomy (gallbladder removal surgery). Most, if not all, these days are done laparoscopically. These *clips* are used in a multitude of surgeries, especially surgeries for women. The health problems in these women were serious enough to force him to operate and remove them. Once removed, the women recovered and were restored to good health. Many, if not all, had their negative and debilitating symptoms disappear completely.

The answer to my pain was directly in front of my eyes, and it seemed so simple. My gallbladder was removed laparoscopically in 2011 by a doctor in Texas. No medical personnel, including the surgeon, informed us that anything was going to be "left" inside of my body. We just simply thought they used dissolvable sutures. When a person goes to the hospital and has an organ removed, the patient is under the belief that nothing foreign or indissoluble will be left inside their body, unless notified. Common sense, right? The burning/stabbing pain that I was experiencing was in the exact spot where my gallbladder used to be. With all the scans of my abdomen, they had to have seen them, right? Why was it so difficult for Western medicine to make the connection?

Now we were in full-blown research mode. I was on our laptop using any and every search engine or website I could find, and Stacy was on her phone doing the same thing. We did not discover anything useful on the Internet regarding health issues relating to the titanium surgical clips. However, we did learn that titanium is not 100 percent pure and usually contains nickel, and nickel is used in the manufacturing process.

People who have nickel allergies commonly develop a rash. Oh, really! Alarm bells sounded, and fireworks exploded above our heads like in the cartoons because our minds were blown. On the Mayo Clinic website, we found numerous pictures of others who had nickel allergic reactions, and a picture of my rash could have been used for their page; they were so comparable. Most of the pictures were from nickel (most likely jewelry) touching the skin and in small areas. Just imagine the rash if the nickel was *inside* of their body. I had a terrible systemic upper torso rash that included my right arm. The clips *had* to be the problem. What else could it be?

My two newly found family members who I had met through that mysterious Facebook message had been instrumental in exposing the hidden information needed to save my life. I continued to communicate with these two *angels* throughout the weekend about the clips, and we learned more about each other. I even spoke with the one who sent the email on the phone, and she told me her story concerning her metal allergy. Her symptoms and story were very different from mine but had the same problematic source—the clips.

Surprisingly, she was getting her clips removed in a few weeks by a surgeon in Austin, Texas. She had her gallbladder removed by the same surgeon one year earlier and was not informed about the clips either. In the past, she had a titanium neck implant removed due to her deteriorating health as a result of her nickel allergy. After the implant was removed, she got much better but not all the way because she had her gallbladder removed with the clips remaining. She even had her blood tested for metal allergies, six hundred dollars all out of pocket. She was nickel positive, and it was proof she needed to make her case for the doctor to do the clip removal surgery.

Certain this was the source of my problem, Stacy and I started making plans for Monday. We were going to show up at all my doctor's offices without an appointment to give our newfound God-inspired diagnosis. The sooner they received the solution, the quicker they could start working on getting these painful clips out of me. *Hopefully*, it would be on Tuesday in place of or during the exploratory surgery.

CHAPTER

11

Leap of Faith

Monday came, and we headed out for our doctor's run. Both the GI and surgeon were in surgeries all day but could be reached intermittently with messages. The surgeon's office said since the exploratory was scheduled for the next day and the preop was not done, we should go immediately to the hospital for them to perform the preop. So we went to the hospital.

Even with the heavy pain meds, I was not feeling good moving around much, and my mood was melancholy and solemn. Stacy had to do all the negotiations and deal with all arrangements with very little input from me. While at the administrator's desk, Stacy's phone rang; it was the surgeon's office, and she immediately answered the phone. The office had spoken with the surgeon and was relaying his response. After hearing about the clips, he said he would have to perform two surgeries. One for exploring and one for removing. After hearing this, Stacy yelled out, "He won't survive two surgeries, much less one!" Her audible level kept increasing as she kept talking.

The panicked administrator looked at me and said, "Please don't make a scene. I've already had one today." By the end of the call, the exploratory surgery was canceled, and we disgustingly left the hospital. In place of the surgery the next day, we had an appointment to see the surgeon at his office.

While we were running around, the angel that first contacted me sent an email to the OB/GYN doctor that wrote the article. She was asking him to "help her brother" by removing my clips or referring me to a surgeon who would remove them. By now, with all the communication between these two angels and myself, they considered me their *brother* from another mother. They wanted to be called sisters from now on.

At the appointment with the surgeon, we were completely and utterly shocked to hear what came out of his mouth. He said, "You were correct to cancel the exploratory because I know how to put the clips in but not how to take them out." Wow, just wow! Why would a surgeon ever put something inside a human body that they don't know how to remove? That just sounded nefarious to me, and then I remembered that doctors are just *practicing* medicine. I was totally floored to hear that come out of his mouth, and I could not speak afterward. I just got up and started walking out of the exam room. I was done with him because he lied in telling us he could do a clip removal surgery after the exploratory.

Now what would we do about pain medication and how do we go about getting the clips removed? We needed help with these issues, so we made an unannounced visit to my family doctor. They worked us in because our visit would not take long. He gave me enough refills for one month but could not agree with our diagnosis because it was totally foreign to anything he knew about Western medicine. Therefore, he had no recommendations or referrals for a clip removal surgeon. Here we go again, our *hope* being squashed and no direction in which to proceed. We prayed for an answer from our Lord. He answered Stacy through an early morning encounter with God on the day moments before we found out about the clips.

During that very spiritual and enlightening experience, she received a sign and word from God. The sign was the beautiful sunrise as she woke before me and went to the front porch for her daily devotional. The word she received was very comforting and specific. She and I were in the "eye of the storm," and He was telling her, "I've got this. Calm down, and don't be afraid or worried about making it through the rest of the storm because I and My angels are going to literally *carry* you through to the conclusion." He was going to make a way where there was no direction or path to visibly see; we were taking a literal "leap of faith" and placing our full trust and faith in Him to lead us. That is a great definition of *hope*, so we placed all we had left in Him.

By this time, the sister who first contacted me received an answer to her email from the OB/GYN doctor who wrote the article. The doctor would not see me personally, but he did refer a surgeon out of Allen, Texas. Awesome! For the first time in ages, I had some positive vibes flowing and started to get a little excited about the possibility of being pain-free. This visit would be different because this surgeon knew about the clips, and we wouldn't have to convince him that they needed to be removed. To our surprise, an expedited appointment was made for the next week.

On the day of the appointment, I had a bad day and felt awful. All the energy I could muster allowed me to lie down. Once in the exam room, I immediately headed toward the table to lie down in the fetal position, and I stayed in that position the whole time. While waiting for the surgeon, I felt uneasy anxiety creeping up on me, and I did not know why. When he entered the room, it was like his ego filled the airspace. He did all the talking during the five minutes he was in the room. It was like a lecture. Paraphrasing, he said, "Medicare had approved your exploratory surgery, and the surgeon only receives four hundred dollars for performing the surgery. Removing the clips is a very dangerous, complex, and life-threatening surgery, and you could die on the table. A major artery runs right next to the surgery area; it could be cut, and you could bleed out. This surgery necessitates a greater payout for the surgeon (me). Give me two weeks to find an insurance billing code that allows me to receive more than four hundred dollars for this surgery. Give me two weeks, and I'll get back to you."

It felt like he was holding my pain hostage for the "all mighty dollar." In my altered mental state, he used scare tactics to make me wait so he could earn more. In an instant, my *hopes* were dashed for a speedy resolution.

CHAPTER 12

The Doctor Will See You Now

"Hurry up and wait." I knew that term all too well when I worked in the oilfield for twenty years. The phone was never far from my side while I impatiently waited for his call. After a week and no call, I decided to check in to get an update. I spoke with his assistant, and he told me the surgeon is most likely going to want me to get blood metal allergy testing. First, we told him in the exam room we could not afford the six hundred dollars out of pocket or the time waiting to have it done. Second, he also saw my rash, and that was my allergy test. Instead of medically helping me, he pushed me away and had me jump through hoops to get care. We never received a phone call back from his office.

Now I was outraged and started texting negative thoughts to anyone who would communicate with me. Where else could I draw *hope* from now besides God? Man and his infinite wisdom had failed me. Western medicine had failed me. Where do I go from here? As the negativity and discouragement poured out of me, God's spirit took hold of my emotions and thought process and reminded me, "I've got this!"

I regained my composer and thought aloud, "Here we go again."

I got a response from my text rant, and it was the sister who just had her clips removed. She was doing her best to comfort me and calm me down. She started out by saying she was feeling much, much better after her clips had been removed, and it had been only a little over a week. "Hold on, just a little longer," she said. Her two-week follow-up appointment with the surgeon who removed her clips was in five days, and she was going to personally speak with him about me. Showing him in person how much better she was doing would make a dramatic impact on him to possibly see me, and *hopefully* very soon. What a godsend that would be! A smile came across my face considering her compassion for me and her voluntary commitment to help me.

The burning/stabbing pain was not subsiding or diminishing and now seemed to be draining my lifeforce. My color had changed to a pale white, and my appearance resembled that of a "dead man walking." My weight had been slowly falling off my frame because my appetite was nonexistent and had been for months. The only real nutrition I got was from Stacy-supplied supplements. Stacy and Markus knew something must happen soon, or I might just collapse and/or pass away at any given moment. Time crept by as I painfully, yet expectantly awaited her appointment day communication.

Wednesday, her appointment day, was here, and the phone had not left my side in anticipation of her correspondence. She contacted me and told me to call her surgeon's office and schedule an appointment. I called the surgeon's office, and shockingly, they were expecting my call. Before they would set an appointment up, the office requested my insurance information, and the surgeon requested I send my latest Cat scan results and my 2011 gallbladder removal surgery operative report. No problem, we already had the operative report and sent it right away. We contacted the family doctor to expedite the Cat scan. Within a couple of hours after sending the requested information, the surgeon's office called me back. Yes, they called me back! She said the surgeon would see me. Hooray! I had an office appointment for next Tuesday, and the removal surgery was tentatively scheduled for the next day—the day before Thanksgiving. Praise the Lord!

What would doctors do these days unless being touched by the Holy Spirit? He has never seen me, doesn't know me, and only heard of me through the word of someone else. He scheduled a surgery, and he hadn't even seen me yet. Talk about unbelievable! Who, what, where? Now everything was happening at lightning speed. God promised He would "carry us," and this was an incredible display of Him putting that guarantee into action.

Stacy's brain was working, mine not so well. She was already thinking ahead about where and how to afford to stay in another city and traveling five hours to get there for my surgery. I was texting the sisters and updating them with the fantastic news; and the first one who contacted me insisted we stay at her house before, during, and after the surgery since she lived in the same city as the surgeon. Just a coincidence, right? Only God could perform such a fantastic feat! Just think, we will be spending Thanksgiving Day with *family* we have never met, in a house we've never set foot inside.

When I updated my pastor, he said what God had orchestrated sounded like a script for a Hallmark movie. In the following months, we would hear that same response many times after sharing our testimony.

Next was how would we transport me to the sister's house and the surgery. At that time, I was of little to no use for driving, and Stacy could make the five-hour trek. But because of her anxiety and fibromyalgia, she would need a few days to recover afterward. God had previously planned for this situation when Markus came to live with us. Once Markus heard of the surgery, unannounced to us, he requested time off from work to be our chauffeur for the entire trip. What a blessing it is to have a godly son!

Everything was being worked out in my favor by the creator of the universe—just wow! All details were being solved without our input. Stacy and I were blown away! In my condition, I could not totally absorb the magnitude of what was taking place on my behalf. God was "carrying" me to the point where I didn't even need to utilize my legs. With the pain intensifying, assistance from Him and His angelic army was crucial to my survival.

The pain was near or at the excruciating point, and my health was deteriorating rapidly, and everyone knew it but me. The four hours between pain pills decreased to three hours, but the fear of addiction was far from my thoughts. My focus was not on the pain because this same pain had been escalating and torturing me for eighteen months now. Being unhealthy or overdosing was not a high priority as the pain and its cause had taken over and were in charge. I totally abandoned control of my health and my life completely to God, Stacy, and Markus.

The gifts of salvation are many, but my favorite and the most comforting is the *hope* of heaven. When my health was declining to near death from fighting GP and struggling mightily with the clips, I never really felt afraid of leaving the earth and entering eternity. The reassurance of knowing *where* I would be going and *who* I would be with doesn't make heaven sound bad by any means. Holding hands of passed loved ones again while walking streets of gold with Jesus on the way to a mansion would be pain-free in my new heavenly body. The loved ones left behind who are missed immensely would now be seen again through His gift of salvation.

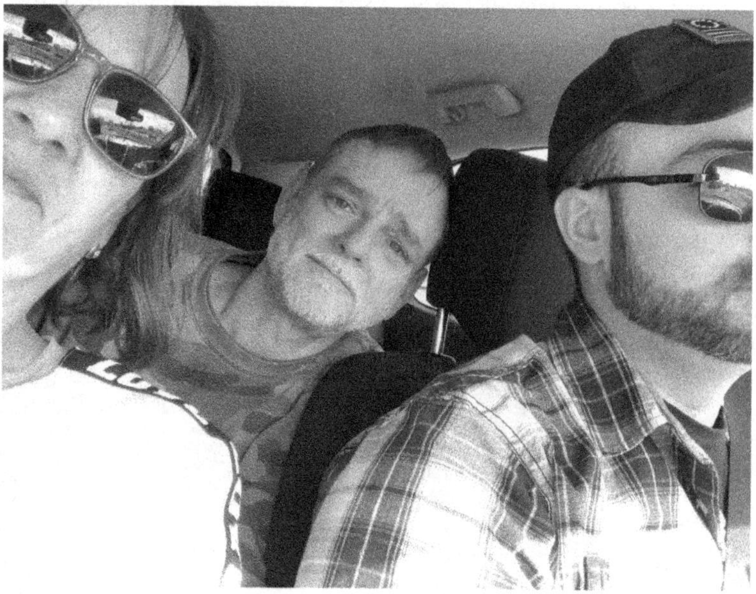

CHAPTER 13

In God's Hands

Travel day arrived, so Stacy and Markus packed the car and loaded me up in the backseat, and off we went on a lifesaving journey. I slept for most of the five-hour voyage to our new family's house. Upon arrival, anxiety that should have accompanied meeting someone new for the first time was stripped away due to the importance of the event. The warm welcome we received from our new family was overwhelming. They treated us like we had been part of their family for decades, not just first-time acquaintances. We fellowshipped like we knew each other our entire lives. The conversation continued well into the evening until my energy ran out. But I had a very important appointment the next day and needed rest.

Believe me, verbal exchanges burn energy, and I can get worn out just communicating with others. Having a lengthy discussion with someone would consume more calories than I had available and force me to take a break before I could continue talking. I had a lot to say and was very passionate when speaking, so not being able to continue was tough for me.

Markus did a great job as our chauffeur around town for the medical appointments and during the whole trip. He was much more than a taxi driver; besides being our one and only son, he supported both of us with unspoken emotional encouragement that kept us from totally falling apart. We arrived on time for all appointments, including the most important one—the first meeting with the surgeon.

The surgeon was very young, friendly, and compassionate. He could not believe how bad I looked nor understand how other doctors had allowed me to deteriorate this far with no answers. He informed us as to his *normal* operating procedures concerning a surgery of this type. Only having done one other surgery of this nature on my sister who told him about me, he would have required blood metal allergy testing. But after one look at my systemic rash, he considered that a positive test. At one point during our office visit, he made me believe he was second-guessing doing my surgery the next day. He said typically he would *not* do surgery on a guess or whim, and we really had no medical proof the clips were the cause of my pain or allergy testing results.

I started weeping and pleading with him that I would die if he didn't do it. He could see my tearful panic and desperation, so he moved closer to me and touched me on the shoulder. He said in a compassionate voice, "I'm going to do the surgery tomorrow, so don't worry." The weeping increased but with a different tone; now tears of relief and gratefulness leaked from my face. He told us he was going to do the exploratory surgery of the complete abdomen *and* take the clips out. He mentioned I might be a little sore because every organ in my abdomen would be moved and inspected. He looked at me empathetically and said, "Get some rest, and I'll see you tomorrow."

Because of my weakened condition, he decided he would do the preop before the surgery tomorrow. They gave us the preop instructions and made the final arrangements for the surgery with the hospital. Since time was of the essence, they billed it as an exploratory surgery as Medicare had already approved it. They required zero payment before the surgery, which was a huge blessing because of our fixed income.

Finally, no more waiting, no more guessing, no more doctors, no more tests, no more burning/stabbing pain! We knew this was the source of my pain because God brought us the information through miraculous ways that no man could have arranged. Western medical doctors had nineteen months to correctly diagnose the source of my pain and were ready to open me up and look around to *try* to find a cause. There was still no guarantee provided that the exploratory, without removing the clips, would uncover the solution. God knew I could not wait for mankind's medical knowledge to discover the origin of my pain before I perished, so He acted to save my life.

On the day of the surgery, God gave me peace and spiritually spoke within me to "fear not." I was calm but mostly numb from the continued heavy pain medication, and the surgical staff was compassionate and accommodating. One of the first tasks the staff performed was a simple X-ray of the gallbladder area to ensure the clips existed before going any further. They also did an electrocardiogram as part of the preop to ensure my heart could handle the surgery. Everything was set for a 1:30 p.m. surgery, so they finished prepping me.

One major request I made to the surgeon and surgical staff was to preserve the clips he removed because they were my "kryptonite," and I sought to retain them. They had no issues with the request and told us we could pick them up at the pathology department of the hospital when we returned for the surgeon's follow-up appointment in two weeks.

There were three specific memories I had from the surgery preop room. First, this was the first time I had ever experienced heated gowns. I had lost so much weight; I got chilled very easily. Hospitals were notoriously cold, and I believed the reason was to minimize germs from growing. The gown's temperature was controlled by a handheld thermostat which allowed it to be very cool to very warm. Fantastic! Second, before the nurse inserted the IV needle for surgery, she used a numbing agent to greatly lessen the sting. Awesome! The IV needle used for surgery was usually a gauge or two larger because of the potential quantity and types of medications utilized during an operation.

Finally, I will never forget the look Markus gave me while I was lying in bed during the surgery preop. When our eyes met, he gazed at my face as if he was trying to imprint every square inch into memory so as to never forget. I truly believe he thought there was a very good chance he would never see me alive again. Markus truly believed God was on my side, but he had witnessed his dad almost die once fighting GP, and this time was much worse. He was deeply concerned and had some serious doubts about me surviving the surgery because he had never seen me this weak and feeble. The peace that I received from God had me try to ease his worry by saying, "Everything is going to be all right, son. Don't worry. God's got this." He never told me if what I said gave him comfort or strength, but I believe my calmness before surgery relieved some of his worrisome mind.

Again, I had given all to God and was ready for whatever He decided for my life; it was out of my hands. I *hoped* for a good outcome but did not trust the industry. However, I did trust the surgeon's expertise in performing the operation because he had done it before, albeit only once. The peace from God conquered all my emotions and thought processes. Even the almost two-hour delay did not ruffle my feathers as nothing could dent my peaceful feeling.

They wheeled me into the operating room (OR), and I was trying to stay awake as long as I could to observe the da Vinci robot setup. My surgeon utilized the da Vinci surgical system; it is a robotic laparoscopic surgical system that uses a minimally invasive surgical approach. There were no major incisions or scars, just four small holes. The surgeon climbed into what looked like an arcade video game console with joysticks, and the robot was feet away and moved into place over an operating table. The apparatus looked like something out of a science fiction movie, but I was not intimidated. I remember hearing a kind angelic voice say, "We are going to take great care of you."

I replied, "I'm cold," because the metal surgical table felt like it was three degrees above freezing. I could see them trying to put me to sleep quickly after that statement, so I started to pray. I thanked Him for His strong arms carrying me here to this point and His unlimited provision for making the way where there was no way visible. Even with IV pain medication up until the point of surgery, I still had the same burning/stabbing pain although it was greatly reduced as I prayed myself into slumber.

As I groggily awoke, I thanked the Lord and felt different from the onset. I was obviously in pain but not the same pain as before. This discomfort was soreness from the four robot incisions, not from the gallbladder area. The burning/stabbing excruciating pain was gone completely, and I started joyfully crying out loud. The postop nurse quickly moved in my direction to check on me, only to discover my outburst was from happiness, not distress.

Once Stacy saw me in postop for the first time, she started to cry jubilantly. The first was because her husband survived the surgery. Second, because of my color and facial expression, she instantly knew the surgery had been successful. She asked me how I felt, and I replied, "Different." It was a *good* different because I certainly did not feel worse than before the surgery. The incisions hurt on the skin's surface, but the agony from within had disappeared. In fact, with all the soreness from the surgery, I still felt less pain and discomfort than what the clips had produced. We both wept together and thanked God for bearing the load of our sorrow, hearing our prayers, and "carrying" us through the remainder of this tribulation season.

It's nothing to be proud of, but we are veterans when it comes to abdominal surgeries. Stacy has had many laparoscopic surgeries because of her endometriosis. In her opinion, the most favorable item needed after abdominal surgery is a pillow, and she's right. A pillow placed over the stomach and held somewhat tightly was of great comfort. It softened the blow of anything that touched the area on the outside and kept everything tight on the inside which minimized the usage of the abdominal muscles. We had one ready for me to use when I left postop.

When we returned to the sister's house, besides my pillow, she noticed the major difference in the way I entered through her front door. There was as she called it "more giddyap in my step" after the surgery. She and her husband were astonished at the drastic change in my character and countenance. The permanent frown that had been on my face since we met had vanished. They enjoyed visiting with a "different person" until the aftereffects from surgery caught up with me, and I grew weary. We all went to bed early because the next day was Thanksgiving. I had a restful pain-free sleep as long as I stayed still and didn't turn over.

For me, this Thanksgiving was special on many different levels. Appreciative to God for being alive would obviously top the list. I was very grateful for the unconditional love and kindness shown by my new family when we were in need. Also, I was thankful to be sharing a meal with strangers who became *family* in the blink of an eye. Many other new family members attended the Thanksgiving meal, and we gave thanks to God for bringing us all together under miraculous circumstances.

There were many great engaging conversations, but one was specially arranged by God because He wanted me to hear the story behind my sisters searching for their brother's relatives (me). The two sisters who started the ancestry search for their adopted sister felt *pushed* to expedite the hunt. They sensed there was a great urgency to their pursuit of their sister, but they had no idea why. Once they found me, the reason for the *push* was made perfectly clear. God and His spiritual realm had been influencing and inspiring them to locate me with the information required to save my life. Every time I reflect on that statement, it brings tears to my eyes.

Even when we don't feel God's presence, He is near. When we don't believe God is hearing our prayers or answering them, He IS listening and acting on our behalf behind the scenes to fulfill His purpose for our lives. God sees our hearts and knows what our faith is built upon. If we give Him time to assemble all the parts necessary to complete His miracle, we will receive a life-changing event to be cherished forever. Trusting that God is executing a miracle for us *right now* as we struggle through a trial or tribulation would be my definition of hope. He has a plan, and it will be accomplished. Sometimes He must carry us to fulfillment; all we must do is ask.

The evening winded down, and everyone was full of the delicious food consumed and filled with delightful fellowship. Some didn't want the day to end, especially me, because, for the first time in several years, I was engaged and animated while conversing. We reminded everyone of our return trip in two weeks for the follow-up appointment with the surgeon. It was imperative that we come back and see the surgeon in two weeks, so he could see for himself the difference he made by removing my clips.

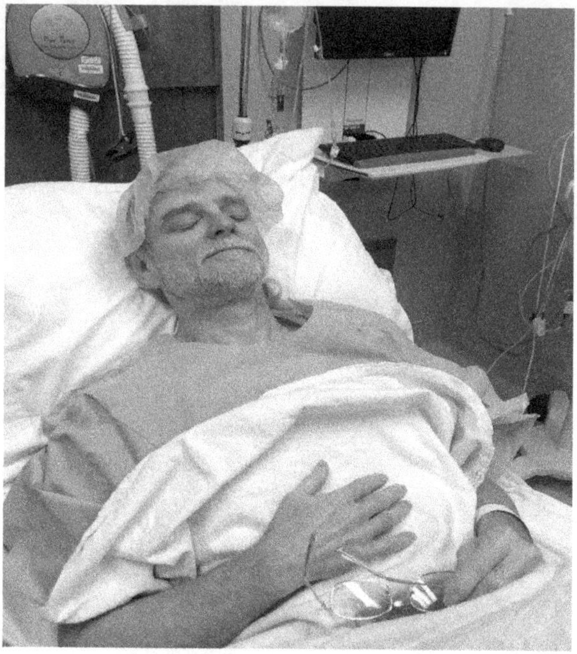

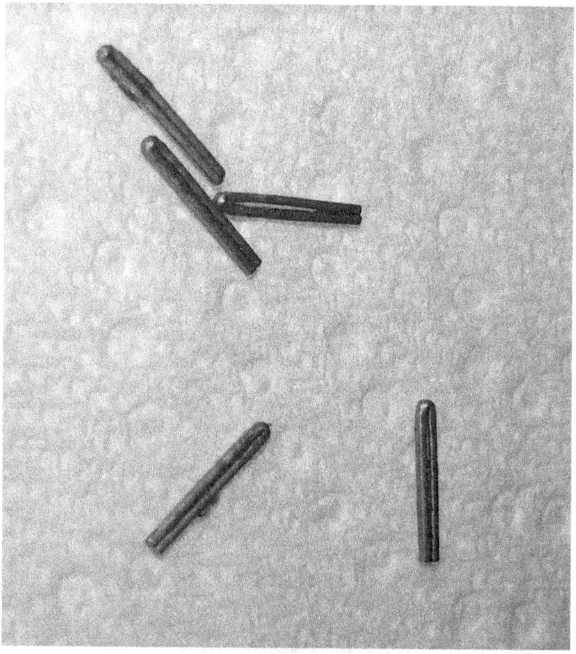

CHAPTER 14

Restoration of Hope

What a difference two weeks made when the foreign object culprits doing the damage to my health were removed and my body was allowed to heal. The rash had not diminished much, but there were no new sores or lesions appearing. My color had completely come back to its normal shade and wasn't pale white. The negative and pain-stricken mood was fading away quickly and being replaced with hopeful optimism for a healthy future. Even with my lack of appetite, I was still gaining weight, energy, and strength.

As a matter of fact, I had gained enough fortitude that we decided I could drive the five hours to see the surgeon. I hadn't driven anything in months, so besides being proud about my progress in my ability to drive, excitement also tingled inside of me just like a teenager to *get* to operate a vehicle again. We made it a relaxing excursion this time, unlike the first trip. Markus did not see the urgency to help us with the driving this time because Stacy wasn't overstressed, and I was basically alive again.

We were greeted with smiles and open arms from my sister as we stayed at her house again. This visit was much shorter but not less enjoyable. The stay was only for a night as we were traveling straight home after the follow-up appointment and picking up the clips. She and her husband were totally amazed at the continued transformation of my health from the first time they encountered me and my broken-down body. We fellowshipped throughout the evening on the miraculous works of God. I stressed how He used two *angel* sisters who answered His calling to literally save my life. Neither sister liked being called an angel, but I explained to them the definition of an angel. An angel is a messenger from God and a kind, good, or beautiful person. They both "fit the bill" on that description. The next morning, we thanked them for their caring generosity and loving hospitality that we could never repay as we tearfully drove away to our appointments.

Since we had a little time before the surgeon's appointment, we traveled to the hospital to pick up the clips. Once we finally found the pathology department within the hospital, it was easy as one-two-three to sign a form and receive my clips. There they were six little tarnished staple-like surgical clips in a plastic container—my "kryptonite." Just looking at them made me believe it was a mistake to leave them behind in my body. Sad to say for me, it wasn't an error.

Next was the follow-up with the surgeon. Wouldn't he be surprised when he saw me? Walking to his office building from the parking garage seemed very strangely different because, this time, I had a "giddyap in my step" as my sister had said. The surgeon was shocked to see me walk into the exam room. He told us when he saw my name on the daily schedule, he speculated if I would be returning in a wheelchair. He continued to say when he removed the clips that there was no infection or sign of abnormality surrounding them. There was only minimal scar tissue throughout the gallbladder area, and after eight years, he expected much more. The exploratory did not expose any irregularity of the organs or the abdominal cavity. He did not believe he helped me in any way medically. He did not find anything that could be responsible for the level and type of pain I was experiencing. At the conclusion of the surgery, he felt all he did was remove the clips. That was enough for me. My surgeon was a very intelligent and highly trained medical professional, yet he did not understand why I was doing much better. But I knew.

Stacy and I told him he was an answer to prayers, and we don't believe he totally understood the impact he had on God's plan. I believe he was complying with the leading from the Holy Spirit to perform this miracle surgery for me. Sometimes an explanation or comprehension of such a spirit-led act is never achieved. However, the outcome is always spirit-revealed, and the person who receives the miracle knows in their hearts that God answered their prayers for help. To this day, I wonder if the surgeon realizes God performed a miracle through him. Nevertheless, God gets *all* the credit!

All the way home, God was smiling because we talked about Him and His influence in our lives and the lives of others around us. I had crossed the point of lost *hope* during this tribulation season. God exposed His authority over the universe to orchestrate an incredible lifesaving plan by utilizing a host of angels. Angelic human believers who answer His call for action permit us to see Jesus working in the lives of others, which also strengthens our *hope*. The difficult concept to grasp is how He uses nonbelievers in His plan also. When I was in pain, the nonbelievers angered and discouraged me but also forced me to depend more on God because I felt that man had failed me. Focusing on Him distracted me from my pain and exposed the level of my faith for others to witness.

When we arrived home, we updated the sisters and other loved ones concerning the follow-up visit with the surgeon. Everyone was very elated just to know I was doing much better, and now my body could heal from the damage done by the poisonous clips. But before my body could completely heal, I had to wean myself off the heavy pain pill usage I was on for over a year. The family doctor told Stacy to bring me in so he could assist us with a weaning schedule that would ensure no addiction withdrawal. We believe opiates caused my GP, so we had experienced not receiving weaning help from a medical professional in the past. The complete story of exploring my GP and surrendering everything to God is uncovered in my other book, *Total Surrender*.

The family doctor was happy to see me and to get a health update from us. During the visit, Stacy mentioned that if the clips had not been removed, she would've been planning a funeral before the end of the year. The doctor immediately replied, "Yup!" With tears in my eyes, it finally hit me! The look on my face was a total shock because I realized for the first time how much my health had deteriorated and that I was knocking on heaven's door. He displayed a chart of my weight and the steady decline for the last two years. The titanium surgical clips were killing me very slowly, but he would not totally agree with the clips being the sole problem source.

After nineteen months, he could not offer any other diagnosis or possible treatment to remedy the source of my pain. He had a very thick binder with my medical records containing all the evidence and testing, yet how could it not have been clear to him? So in my view, his credibility was in question because his medical training had altered his thinking. He would no longer be able to help me with the leftover symptoms from the clips because he didn't totally believe they were the problem source. God angelically handed the information for the solution to us, so my *faith* and *hope* were in Him to continue healing my body and soul. Praise the Lord! I'm alive, and the *hope* found within me is strong!

What is your kryptonite? What is causing you to lose *hope*? It could be something that you have done or something that was done to you even without your knowledge. Possibly, it could be a foreign object inside of your body that's causing a chemical change in your brain and therefore affecting your whole being. And maybe, you don't even know it is there. Without my Holy Spirit—filled faith in God's promises and my conviction to follow Jesus, I know deep in my heart my existence would be in heaven and in the memories of my friends and loved ones.

Place your *hope* and faith in God because man does not know all the answers to the Lord-formed created-from-dirt human body. My "quest for hope" took me to and from the lowest point in my life where no hope existed, or could be found in mankind or on the earth. My hope firmly exists in God alone. Amen!

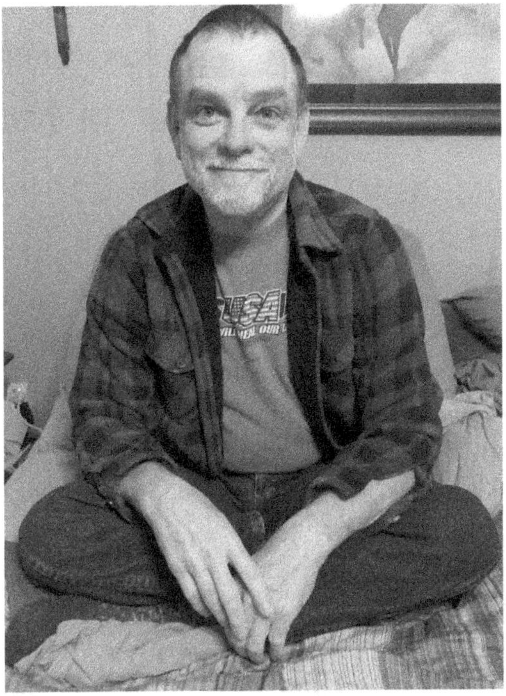

CHAPTER 15

Stacy's Reflections on Her Personal Quest for Hope

My hope and trust in God have been solidified by the many trials and struggles experienced throughout my life. Being a *caregiver* to a chronically ill person is difficult enough on its own. However, doing so while suffering from a chronic disease myself puts it on a whole new level. It is my hope that my insights and valuable lessons acquired while caring for my husband will help others who are experiencing a difficult trial or season of life.

Remember, God does not waste *any* experience or part of our lives to bring us closer to Him. Some of these experiences come by His design while others occur as consequences of our actions, *but* they all come with His permission *and* are filtered through His fingers of love. The Lord has gone before us and buried a valued treasure or stored a rich truth in every trial or tribulation. We, as Christians, strive to keep ourselves in His light; however, these specific truths can only be absorbed in darkness and despair.

> And I will give you the treasures hidden in the darkness—secret riches. I will do this so you may

know that I am the LORD, the God of Israel, the one who calls you by name. (Isaiah 45:3 NLT)

When our distressed hearts are breaking, and we have questions—questions we do not have answers for—God invites us to discuss our troubling questions with Him. The answers that we seek are beyond our comprehension and too heavy of a burden for us to carry alone. When we totally "hand over" the answers to Him, it comforts us to know the burdensome outcome is safe with Him, and He will be glorified in the resolution. God cares about everything that concerns our lives, everything that grieves our hearts. Amid our darkness, He is our hope, the One we can trust.

Unlike any other human feeling, experiencing extreme suffering has a way of equipping us to be the best expressions of God's compassion and grace. When we have faced pain and misery on a physical level, it enables us to love and care for others in ways that are helpful and beneficial, not harmful or detrimental. A caretaker or healer who has not been physically afflicted is extremely limited in their abilities to participate in the caretaking or healing of others, especially mentally (2 Corinthians 1:3–7).

Watching someone you love dearly spiral down the dark pit of despair and depression as their physical health declines is a tremendously heart-wrenching event to witness. The physical and mental toll experienced by the caretaker ultimately preparing for their loved ones looming imminent death is unbearable without Christ. I am very grateful for the lessons learned and the mercy shown by our loving and caring Father God. He never ceases to amaze me with His reassuring love and calming peace during the scariest of storms and the darkness of tribulations.

During this season of caretaking for Mark and his battle to survive, there were countless times of tearful episodes on the side of the road in the car or in the bathroom alone with the door closed that were not witnessed by anyone. This was to not allow my anguish and distress to be visible to Mark or Markus. I simply could not let them see how scared I was about our uncertain future. I thought his first battle with gastroparesis was difficult, but this health crisis was much worse. It was during these dark times alone with God when He spoke to me the loudest.

No matter how low my emotions got, He would send some sort of encouragement to remind me of His presence. The message would be in the form of something as simple as a brightly colored redbird or as majestic as a brilliant sunrise of His making. Often, I received comfort from my sister, Marilyn, who allowed me to escape briefly through numerous trips to Sonic when the situation felt unbearable.

There were also times when I shamed myself because of the many chores that were left undone due to the time spent being near Mark. The beneficial impact on us was immeasurable versus whatever household tasks were not performed. The healing love felt through the closeness of holding hands while watching a movie or just lying next to him while he was sleeping could not be valued enough at the time. The uncompleted chores are not what will be remembered but the special moments spent with the loved one will.

It wasn't until I was able to let go of my selfish desires of keeping Mark with me under any circumstance and let God know I was willing to accept His outcome whatever it may be that I felt true peace—His peace. The hardest prayer to make is one in which you ask God to end a loved one's suffering by taking them home to heaven, knowing it means you will no longer have them by your side. That is exactly what I did, and God restored my hope for our future. My hope and faith in Christ continue to strengthen each day.

Personal lessons and insights

- The way to feel peace during a troubling situation is by staying filled with the power of the Holy Spirit (Romans 15:13).
- Storms in life are inevitable. When you survive a storm, you now have gained the experience and knowledge to help others weather their storm.
- Nothing that happens in our lives surprises God. Every event, conversation, joy, and sorrow—He has either planned or allowed all of them to occur. Everything is fil-

tered through God's hands. Jesus knew that life on this planet would include trials, pain, heartaches, and challenges because He underwent them all.
- God grows our faith through hardships and adversities. He desires for us to live a life of spiritual, emotional, and relational wholeness—a thriving life that, in turn, enables us to withstand the difficulties and struggles of living on a fallen planet.
- Do not get ahead of God. Everything He does is by His timely appointment, and the reason is not usually clear to us mortals because His ways are not our ways. God has scheduled a time to fulfill His promise to us, and He always keeps His promises. So do not be impatient for the Lord to act on your behalf.
- When God does not seem to do what you necessarily want at the time you want—He is doing something better. "Many are the plans in a person's heart, but it is the LORD's purpose that prevails" (Proverbs 19:21).
- When the storms of life happen, the only solid foundation we can count on is God's Word. The Bible is eternal, unchanging, and promises us a hope and a future (Jeremiah 29:11).
- How we respond to the storms and/or pain is our choice. We can surrender to the agonizing darkness or embrace the pain and learn from it. We can try to ignore the pain and hope it all goes away, or we can face it and allow God to heal the broken places.
- Take the time to heal your body physically, mentally, and spiritually. Healing from excruciating suffering is not simply returning to how we were before the event but becoming better than we would have been without ever living through the experience. Our circumstances do not always change for the better, but we can be confident that God will utilize them to change *us* for the better.

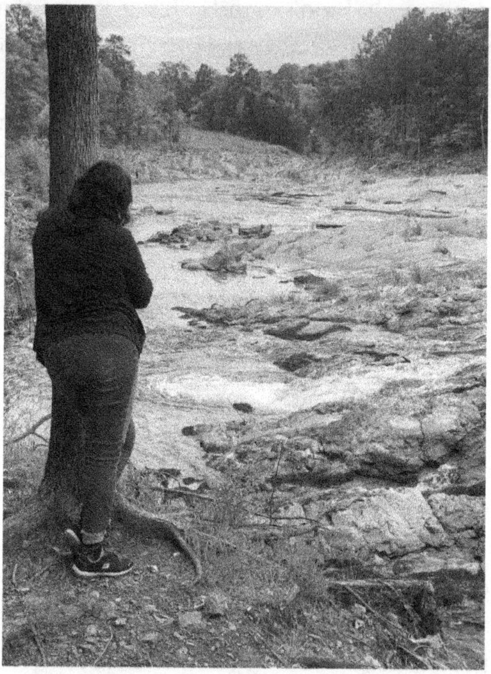

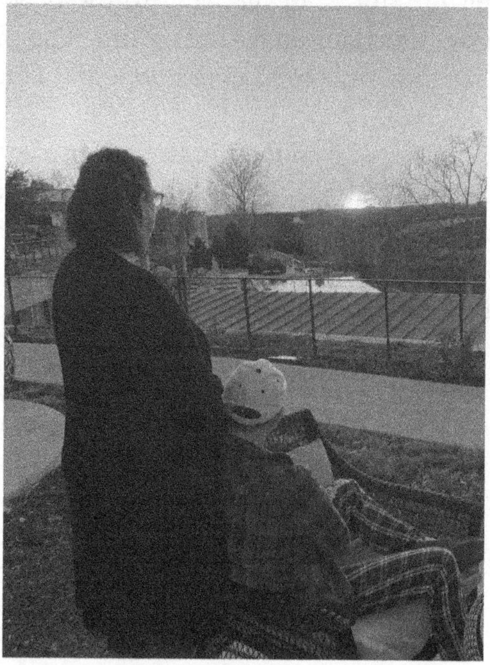

About the Author

Mark Craber is a devout Christian husband and father who has lived his *Green Acres* moment by moving from Houston, Texas, to Kenefic, Oklahoma. Before being medically disabled, through experiences learned from working twenty years in the oilfield, he owned and operated an electrical service business for fourteen years with his wife of forty years, Stacy. God provided this livelihood to allow homeschooling for their son, Markus. Their *tight* family bond would be instrumental in his fight for life and answers from the Western medical industry. During his *quest for hope* experience, he found that some answers can only come from God.

Author Contact: walkingwithchrist220@gmail.com